Healing Plants of the Bible

Their Uses Then and Now

Tim Morrison, DMin, ND

PublishAmerica

Baltimore

First printing

ISBN: 1-59129-522-X
PUBLISHED BY PUBLISHAMERICA BOOK
PUBLISHERS
www.publishamerica.com
Baltimore

Printed in the United States of America

Table of Contents

Section III: Appendices

Acknowledgements

There are several individuals whom I want to publicly acknowledge for their help and encouragement in this journey. I must begin with Dr. Andrew Z. Linial, Jr., friend and colleague, who encouraged me to enter the field of alternative medicine as a profession. Andy had a vision and helped me take ownership of it. Aromatherapist Naomi Uesaka became a vital, energetic and trusted friend in this journey. Naomi shared her personal library with me and always was ready with a word of encouragement.

Last, but certainly not least of all, my heartfelt gratitude abounds for my family. For the majority of their years on earth, my sons, Joel and Sean, could always say, "My dad is a minister." That was clear and succinct. Now they say, "Well, he is a body-mind-spirit coach, a doctor of naturopathy, a spiritual director, a naturopathic counselor and a writer." They cheer me on in my journey. Marta, my wife, partner and the love of my life, has endured my "mid-life crisis" of career change, the struggles and challenges of my dreams, and has encouraged me all the way. To her I am exceedingly grateful and deeply indebted.

Choosing the Revised Standard Version of Scripture

The Revised Standard Version (RSV) translation of the scripture is used in this book. References, for the most part, do not include the apocryphal writings. Ecclesiasticus is referenced several times. Ecclesiasticus is accepted as canon in the Roman Catholic tradition and as apocryphal in the Reformation tradition. Ecclesiasticus is cited because several authors referred to it.

The RSV was selected because this writer has his greatest familiarity with it. Choosing a specific translation for this work was essential in order to establish a standard of reference. Words can and do vary according to translations and/or interpretations. A *translation* is an attempt to recreate in another language (English), word-for-word, the scriptures from the original Greek or Hebrew. An *interpretation* is an attempt to gather and reproduce the *meaning* of the scriptures.

Consider these examples:

Matthew 23.23

King James Version (KJV, a translation): "Woe unto you, scribes and Pharisees, hypocrites! For ye pay tithe of mint and *anise* and *cummin* ..."

Revised Standard Version (RSV, a translation): "Woe to you, scribes and Pharisees, hypocrites! For you tithe mint and *dill* and *cummin* ..."

New English Bible (NEB, an interpretation): "Alas for you, lawyers and Pharisees, hypocrites! You pay tithes of mint and *dill* and *cummin* ..."

Today's English Version (TEV, an interpretation): "How terrible for you, teachers of the Law and Pharisees! You hypocrites! You give to God one tenth even of the seasoning herbs, such as mint, *dill* and *cumin* ..."

These four versions of the same verse indicate three that use dill and one (KJV) that uses anise. The RSV does not use the word anise at all throughout its translation. Three versions make no use of the word herbs, while one (TEV) does. Three of the four spell cummin with two "m's" (as in ancient times), while the TEV uses the modern spelling of cumin with only one "m."

Isaiah 35.1
KJV: "The wilderness and the solitary place shall be glad for them; and the desert shall rejoice, and blossom as the *rose.*"
RSV: "The wilderness and the dry land shall be glad, the desert shall rejoice and blossom; like the *crocus* ..."
NEB: "Let the wilderness and the thirsty land be glad, let the desert rejoice and burst into *flower.*"
TEV: "The desert will rejoice, and *flowers* will bloom in the wastelands."

The NEV and TEV speak of flowers blooming. The RSV speaks of blossoming crocuses. The KJV alone mentions rose.

Mark 14.3
KJV: "And being in Bethany, in the house of Simon the leper, as he sat at meat, there came a woman having an alabaster box of *ointment of spikenard* very precious ..."
RSV: "And while he was at Bethany in the house of Simon the leper, as he sat at table, a woman came with an alabaster jar of *ointment of pure nard*, very costly ..."
NEB: "Jesus was at Bethany, in the house of Simon the leper. As he sat at table, a woman came in carrying a small bottle of very costly perfume, *pure oil of nard.*"
TEV: "Jesus was in Bethany at the house of Simon, a man who had suffered from a dreaded skin disease. While Jesus was eating, a woman came in with an alabaster jar full of a *very expensive perfume*

8

made of pure nard."

In the KJV and some other older translations, the ointment or oil is referred to as "spikenard." The RSV and the other more modern or recent translations use the word "nard." The difference in name arises from the translations of the early texts. In the Greek text, a word which means pure, genuine or liquid, modifies the word nard. The Vulgate modified nard with the word *spicatus*, which refers to the spike-like form of the root and lower stem of the young plant. The Greek speaks of pure nard or genuine nard; however, tradition and repeated usage resulted in the term spikenard. [Curiously, "computer spellcheck" does not recognize "nard" but does recognize "spikenard." Similarly, spellcheck does not recognize "cummin" but does recognize "cumin."]

Given these examples of word variance based upon translation, one can understand the importance of selecting a specific translation/ interpretation/version of the scripture for consistency in research and presentation. Careful selection may subsequently eliminate consideration of a word or substance one might believe to be in the Bible. In this instance, as shown in the example above, anise will not be discussed. Also, spikenard will be referred to as nard.

Note:

In keeping with standard practice, the abbreviation LXX is used to refer to the Septuagint. Septuagint is the name generally given to the oldest Greek version of the Old Testament. The term *septuaginta* (seventy) is based on the ancient tradition that seventy elders accompanied Moses up the Mount and saw the God of Israel. God then gave the tables of the law to Moses, and the seventy elders became responsible for translating the Torah into Greek. An occasional reference also is made to the Vulgate. The Vulgate is a Latin version of the Bible prepared by St. Jerome in the fourth century. The Vulgate served as an authorized version of the scripture for the Roman Catholic Church.

Introduction

At the beginning of my working life, never in my wildest imagination would I have predicted that I would write this book. At that time, however, I was not in the field of alternative medicine. This manuscript emerged out of a research project during my studies in naturopathy. With two seminary degrees and an ongoing interest in scripture study, I knew I would enjoy researching one of the suggested topics, "The Use of Essential Oils in the Scriptures."

My interest in this field actually had its origin in 1978. From August, 1978 to August, 1981, I lived and worked as an educator in the bush village of Peki, Volta Region, Ghana, West Africa. When I left the United States for Ghana, I took with me an enormous supply of over-the-counter medications and some prescription medicines as well. I packed these with the hope that they would carry me through my three-year term of service. However, I soon found myself relying upon local medicines instead. These medicines were made from grasses, herbs, roots, and some things that my Ghanaian friends told me I really did not want to know about! I always used these local cures and treatments and actually began to request the local remedy when I needed a curative.

During those three years, I recall receiving an issue of a weekly news magazine in which the cover story dealt with "alternative medicine." I laughed as I read the article for what the cover story called alternative medicine was "everyday, traditional medicine" in Peki and throughout Africa; in fact, as I came to learn, throughout much of the world.

Since leaving Ghana in 1981, I have returned on four separate occasions to lead work tours for groups of individuals. During each of those two-week adventures, when travelers experienced nausea or diarrhea or some other common ache or pain, I turned time and again to the local medicines. Each time, the local curative worked.

So, what is an essential oil? Jeanne Rose, author of *375 Essential Oils and Hydrosols,* offers this definition: "[Essential oil] is the heart and soul of the plant. It is the essence that deters bugs from eating the plant. It is the fragrant, aromatic heart of the plant that attracts bees and pollinating insects. It is the chemical component contained in tiny plant cells that is liberated during the distillation process."

It is this component in a wide variety of plants—used in Biblical times, and today in ever-increasing numbers—that this book addresses. This book is about natural curatives.

Part I:
Establishing a Foundation

God Saw That It Was Good

A refrain of God as creator courses through the scripture from the opening words of Genesis: "In the beginning God created the heavens and the earth…and God saw that it was good." (Genesis1.1, 10b); to the closing book of Revelation: "And the angel whom I saw standing on sea and land lifted up his right hand to heaven and swore by him who lives for ever and ever, who created heaven and what is in it, and the sea and what is in it…" (Revelation 10.5-6a); and numerous books in between.

"…*and God saw that it was good.*" All that God creates is good, and he has commissioned humankind to use wisely all that he has given, and continues to give, in and through creation.

When I look at thy heavens, the work of thy fingers …
What is man that thou art mindful of him …

Thou hast given him dominion over the works of thy hands;
—Psalm 8.3a, 4a, 6a

Ecclesiasticus 38.4 admonishes: "The Lord created medicines from the earth, and a sensible man will not despise them." Revelation 22.1, "Then he showed me the river of the water of life, bright as crystal, flowing from the throne of God and of the Lamb" brings together images from Genesis and Psalms. Verse 1 calls to mind Genesis 2.10: "A river flowed out of Eden to water the garden, and there it divided and became four rivers" and Psalm 46.4-7, "There is a river whose streams make glad the city of God, the holy habitation of the Most High. God is in the midst of her, she shall not be moved;

God will help her right early. The nations rage, the kingdoms totter; he utters his voice, the earth melts. The Lord of hosts is with us; the God of Jacob is our refuge."

The Tree of Life

Revelation 22.2: "...through the middle of the street of the city; also, on either side of the river, the tree of life with its twelve kinds of fruit, yielding its fruit each month; and the leaves of the tree were for the healing of the nations."

The tree of life has twelve fruits (one ripe fruit for each month), which represent the seasons of life. This tree—one of two specific trees mentioned in Genesis 2—is available for all to eat. From the beginning to nearly the very end, scripture boldly declares that God is the Creator and Lord, and from that declaration emerges the sense that he provides healing for all of his children.

For everything created by God is good,
and nothing is to be rejected if it is received with thanksgiving;
for then it is consecrated by the word of God and prayer.
—I Timothy 4.4-5

Taking God Seriously

History and archaeology indicate that humankind took seriously the exhortation from God to use plants and herbs, the gifts of creation for health and wholeness of humanity. Pictures on the walls of the Lascaux caves of France suggest that flowers, plants and their essences have been used for healing, relaxation and enhanced lovemaking since as far back as 18,000 B.C. However, the preponderance of research supports a date circa 5000 B.C. for the use of flowers, plants and their essences.

Shirley Price and Len Price in their work, *Aromatherapy for Health Professionals,* write, "Plants and their extracts have been used since time immemorial to relieve pain, aid healings, kill bacteria and thus revitalize and maintain good health...although the word [aromatherapy] was not coined until [the 20th century]. The distilled extracts from plants—the essential oils—have been employed by humankind for countless years in religious rites, perfumery and hygiene. Cedarwood oil, known to have been used by the Egyptians for embalming and for hygienic purposes 5,000 years ago, was probably the first 'distilled' oil to have been produced, although the process is open to speculation."

In *Mastering Herbalism: a Practical Guide*, Paul Huson concurs with a history of 5,000 years or more of humanity working with plants and herbs to enhance life, with herbs undoubtedly being used in upper and lower Egypt and Mesopotamia in 3000 B.C. Susanne Fischer-Rizzi in *The Complete Incense Book*, "...[traces] the origin of burning incense—that is, using aromatic substances in burning ceremonies—to the earliest of human history, probably before or during the Stone age." Although not generally "dated," because a cult's movement from Stone age to Bronze age was predicated upon its beginning to use tools of bronze, a rough time frame for the beginning of the Stone age is about 2,500,000 years ago, with an ending time of about 5000 B.C. to 3000 B.C.

* The story of Joseph, son of Jacob, recounts that Joseph's brothers sold him to "…a caravan of Ishmaelites coming from Gilead, with their camels bearing gum, balm and myrrh, on their way to carry it down to Egypt." (Genesis 37.25) Tradition dates this event sometime between 2000 B.C. and 1500 B.C.
* Exodus 25 records the formula for Holy oil.
* Numbers 11 tells of the murmuring of the Hebrews in the wilderness over foods and herbs, which they longed for from their days of slavery in Egypt.
* King Solomon received aromatic gifts from the Queen of Sheba. (I Kings 10; II Chronicles 9)
* The prophet Jeremiah mentions Balm of Gilead (Jeremiah 8) and frankincense (Jeremiah 6,17).

Scanning the writings of the prophets, especially Amos and Micah, we find support for Fischer-Rizzi's declaration that incense burning was critical to our ancestors' sacred purpose of conveying messages to the heavens, helping to carry prayers to the appropriate destination. Incense burning is not an old habit dying out but continues today, even growing in practice to help support individuals in their prayer life and meditation, and deepening their experiences. Medical papyri dating back to circa 1555 B.C. contain remedies for all types of illnesses and the methods of application are similar to ones used in aromatherapy and herbal medicine today. These events and individuals span the years from about 2000 B.C. to around 600 B.C.

Kathi Keville and Mindy Green in *Aromatherapy: a Complete Guide to the Healing Art* cite a 1975 archaeological expedition to the Indus Valley. That expedition found an unusual terra-cotta apparatus that looked like a primitive "still" dating from 3000 B.C., which would place it about 4,000 years earlier than most sources date the invention of distillation. A vessel of similar design from about 2000 B.C., and unquestionably a still, was discovered in Afghanistan. No conflict actually exists in the dating of distillation, as ancient distillation involved the use of the sun as a heat source. Distillation as practiced today did begin around 1000 AD.

Notwithstanding these findings, fixing with certainty the date of the first extraction with distillation that results in what today is called an *essential oil* is difficult at best. The first distillate helped make alcohol from wine. Genesis 9.20-24 tells of Noah becoming drunk when he and all the inhabitants of the ark were finally on dry ground following the flood. Though aromatic herbs, balsams and resins were used for thousands of years to embalm and/or for religious ceremonies or sacrifices, no document provides clear evidence of the preparation of essential oils.

When did essential oils come into use? Were essential oils used by people of Bible times? Are essential oils mentioned in scripture? Given this overview, the response to these three questions would be: Although some essential oils may have come into use in earlier ages by different means of distillation, essential oils as understood and used today did not become cultural features until about 1000 A.D. Therefore, it is exceedingly doubtful that essential oils were used in Biblical times. Hence, essential oils are not mentioned in scripture. Scripture does tell of *balms, resins, gums* and *plants*, which the people used and traded, from which essential oils are made today. These plants, which are mentioned in the Revised Standard Version of the Bible, are discussed in Section II. But before moving onto that discussion, let us first look at the early development of medicine.

God, Healing, and Humankind

Seeking to ease pain is simply a natural human reaction. Individuals want relief from pain and discomfort. The search for that relief could be described as the start of the field of medicine. How close can we describe, define or date that start, except to say that when a human first felt pain or felt ill, at that point the medical journey began.

Primitive humans used common sense: They observed how animals took care of themselves. As best as possible, people noticed how animals cured themselves of wounds or from ailments. By watching these things, primitive humans got ideas on how to care for themselves. Sometimes illnesses were attributed to the actions of unfriendly spirits, demons or ghosts. Magicians and/or priests chanted, prayed, offered sacrifices and suggested rituals to bring release, relief, or healing.

Biblically speaking, we might argue that the origin of medicine began with the fall of humanity. Adam and Eve and their appetites created the situation that called for the eventual emergence of medical science.

History and archaeology do trace back for thousands of years indications of medical practice. The Papyrus Ebers, written around 1500 B.C., contains some information from 3400-2500 B.C. as well as prescriptions from the 6th Egyptian Dynasty, which dates from 2323-2152 B.C.

The Papyrus Ebers contains 811 prescriptions for ailments from a variety of sources. These prescriptions include the names of drugs/plants/materials used, quantities and the method of administering the mixture. There are directions for salves, plasters, poultices, snuffs, inhalations, gargles, draughts, confections, pills, fumigants and enemas. In a very general way, the maladies the Papyrus addresses are those that attack people today: worms due to bad water, skin diseases, ophthalmic problems and infections. Some researchers believe the Papyrus Ebers to be book 40 of the 42 Hermetic books. It was passed around among physicians, helping them to know how to treat patients. As such, the Papyrus established a standard for the practice of medicine at that time.

Many historians cite Imhotep of Egypt as the first known physician. A commoner by birth, Imhotep rose through the ranks of the Egyptian dynasty because of his natural skills, abilities and dedication to his tasks. A good poet, a renowned architect and a priest-physician, Imhotep served under four kings during the 3rd Egyptian Dynasty (2650-2575 B.C.). Imhotep's best-known writings were his medical writings.

The Code of Hammurabi influenced the development of medicine. This code of laws, written around 2250 B.C., encouraged people to accept the authority of a king and to follow the rules, laws and codes for the common good of the people and the nation. Part of the Code contained fees and regulations pertaining to doctors and their successful treatment of patients. The Code also outlined punishments for unsuccessful treatment. The existence of such guidelines within the Code of Hammurabi indicates some level of development for the field of medicine. The fees and regulations acted as an incentive, the punishments as a disincentive.

The presence of doctors in a given culture varied according to the power and presence of magic and superstition. The first Greek historian, Herodotus (484?-425? B.C.) recorded that in his time medicine had deteriorated immensely because of superstition. The Babylonians, Chaldeans and many other nations had no physicians. When a person was ill or attacked by a disease, that person was carried into a public street. There, passersby who had experienced a similar ailment or disease or had witnessed something similar would advise the ailing person to adopt such means as their judgment and memory could suggest. No one was permitted to pass near such a person without talking with the individual about the nature of the suffering or ailment.

Out of this medical milieu emerged Hippocrates (460?-380? B.C.), who became known as the father of medicine as we understand medicine today. Instead of turning to magic or witchcraft or superstition when confronting illness, Hippocrates employed reason. He assumed that diseases had natural causes; therefore, diseases could be studied and observed and then possibly cured according to the workings of nature. He believed that diet, water quality, climate and social environment effected people's health. Hippocrates focused on treating the *whole person* instead of merely isolating and treating symptoms. He reasoned that strong medicines were needed for strong people affected by strong diseases. Weak people needed a different kind of medicine. Hippocrates developed a resource of 400 simple herbal remedies of which 200 continue in use today. Some of the plants, spices and herbs that Hippocrates used were: almond, balm, cinnamon, coriander, wild cucumber, fig, garlic, mallow, mint, myrrh, onion, rose, rue and saffron. Each of these is discussed in Section II.

Although the doctrine of signatures formally appeared in the early 17th century when Jacob Boehme published his book, *Signatura Rerum: the Signature of All Things*, the doctrine emerged virtually from the beginning of time. The Doctrine of Signatures suggests that God marked everything he created with a sign or a signature. The sign indicated the purpose of the item. Humankind looked at a plant, its root, its leaf, its flower and how and where it grew, and then gauged from that collective information what were the plant's concealed curative principles. An example is the iris, whose petals were commonly used as a poultice for bruises because the color of the petals—purple, a signature—resembled the color of the bruises the poultice was to cure.

How did the Israelites develop the medical practices, which are so well laid out in their writings? There is disagreement among scholars. Some argue that Israel learned much from the Babylonians, Persians and Egyptians during their times of captivity. Others argue that the Israelites borrowed very little from those times and cultures.

What *is* clear is that Israelite-Jewish medicine was based on elaborate laws for the prevention of illness. Even the casual reader readily recognizes that the book of Leviticus in the Old Testament is an amazing medical book. Much of the Mosaic law (the guidelines found primarily in Leviticus and Deuteronomy) addressed prevention and suppression of epidemics and diseases, care of skin, combating venereal infection and prostitution, the systematizing of work and calling for Sabbath rest. These law codes on health and sanitary issues made the Jews the healthiest and most macrobiotic of people.

Legends arose amongst the Israelites that King Solomon compiled an herbal lore and a valuable treatise on pharmacopoeia, both of which have vanished. A similar legend is that Solomon wrote a book that instructed how to treat disease by natural means; but the book was destroyed because the use of the remedies pointed out in it could have thwarted the interests of the Levites, who cured diseases by expiatory sacrifices. The historian Josephus wrote "God had accorded [Solomon] the power of appeasing [God's] rage by prayers and of driving impure spirits out of the bodies of the sick by conjurations. This method is the one followed in our day."

Ultimately, *healing* is what God is all about. Exodus 15.26b declares: "...for I am the Lord, your healer." Granted, Old Testament writings present God as using disease as an expression of his wrath, but God does confer both disease and health (Deuteronomy 32.39: "...I kill and I make alive; I wound and I heal ..."; Ecclesiastes 3.3: "a time to kill, and a time to heal; a time to break down, and a time to build up."). God brings healing in response to individual prayers, in response to the pleas and actions of the patriarchs and prophets, in response to the turning of the hearts of the people, and simply because God *chooses* to bring healing. Healing was something that was expected of prophets. Healing was something hoped for by the people.

In *The Uncommon Touch: an Investigation of Spiritual Healing*, author and journalist Tom Harpur writes, "A careful study of the Gospels reveals that their entire message is ultimately about healing— the healing of the individual, of the community, of the whole of humanity. Physical, emotional and mental wholeness are all part of what it means to find salvation." Harpur adds that "Jesus saw fear as the chief enemy of human health and wholeness. His most characteristic sayings are exhortations to his disciples and others to have courage, to 'be of good cheer,' to let go of worry and anxiety and have radical trust in the 'heavenly Father.'"

In his book, *Healing Christianity*, Morton Kelsey declares that Jesus healed because: "[Jesus] cared about people and suffered when they did...[Jesus] was hostile to what made people sick...Jesus healed to help us toward transformation. It was Jesus' ministry to preach, teach and heal." Kelsey also offers these thoughts: "The coming of Jesus, if indeed he was the incarnation of God, wipes out once and for all the notion that God puts sickness upon people because of divine wrath. Jesus' ministry of healing embodies the exact antithesis of this idea. The 'Christian' attitude that glories in sickness is completely alien to that of Jesus of Nazareth; it is aligned on the side of what he was fighting against." These two books—Morton Kelsey's *Healing Christianity* and Tom Harpur's *The Uncommon Touch: an Investigation of Spiritual Healing*—merit reading and consideration by any who seek more knowledge and understanding in spiritual healing and faith.

Jesus sent out his disciples to preach, to teach and to heal (see Mark 6.7, Matthew 10.5-8, Luke 9.1). The disciples were overwhelmed with their success. Jesus also chose 70 others and sent them out to heal the sick (see Luke 10.1-9). In Jesus' great discourse with his disciples in the upper room, Jesus declared, "Truly, truly, I say to you, he who believes in me will also do the works that I do; and greater works than these will he do, because I go to the Father. Whatever you ask in my name, I will do it, that the Father may be glorified in the Son. If you ask anything in my name, I will do it" (John 14.12-14). Healing was a part of the life and ministry of Christ, and he expected healing to continue within the Church.

Since the time of Christ and the apostles, the Christian Church has both helped and hindered the continuance of healing ministries as well as the development of medicine in its many forms. The first Christians were noted for their compassionate care and treatment of the ill among their own and of the ill abandoned by society. Christians' care of the sick helped faith grow. They visited the sick without fear. They extended to the ill the very best of care for Christ's sake. The actions of Christians contrasted sharply with those of non-Christians. The Church even began to sanctify the practice of caring for the sick. Local churches often served as a safe repository for books and writings pertaining to health and healing, which might have been at risk during times of battles and invasions. However, the Church hindered the development of medicine if some new thought or procedure conflicted with official church doctrine. Internal struggles and fighting in the Church created an atmosphere in which some scholars were hesitant to put forth new ideas on medicine. History records incidents in which the Church took deliberate steps to crush science. Today, the Church ultimately stands supportive of medicine through church-related medical facilities, schools of nursing and medical missionaries. Some local congregations encourage within their members the exploration of complementary and alternative medicines, which, paradoxically, are the bedrock of the earliest medicine.

Why These Plants?

There are many books that discuss plants of the Bible. These books literally span centuries. They also vary in the amount of detail presented. The bibliography of this book gives witness to this. The primary focus of this book, however, is not plants but *essential oils*. The plants discussed in this book emerged from a list of essential oils.

That list was developed from lists of essential oils found in Jeanne Rose's *The Aromatherapy Book*, Shirley Price's *Aromatherapy Workbook*, and *The Complete Book of Essential Oils & Aromatherapy* by Valerie Ann Worwood. I simply studied lists of oils/plants offered in these books and traced their references in *Nelson's Complete Concordance of the Revised Standard Version Bible*. Sixty-one words were researched. Not all of the words were a plant or an essential oil. Some were words that are relevant to aromatherapy and to the nature of this book. Two such words are "oil" and "incense," words that one would anticipate finding in writings about people who use plants, gums, resins and their various forms as medicines, incense and fragrances. These additional words are discussed in the appendices, as well as a complete list of the words with their Biblical references.

Two separate and distinct lists can be found in the appendices:

- Biblical references compiled by *word* such as myrrh or coriander, along with the aforementioned discussion of correlative words.
- References compiled by *Book of the Bible*, e.g., Genesis containing one reference to odor, two to oil, two to myrrh and one to almond.

Part II:
The Essential Oils

Almond

When Jacob's (Israel's) sons returned to Egypt to purchase food during the time of famine, Jacob instructed them to take "some of the choice fruits of the land" as a present to the ruler. That list of choice fruits included almonds (Genesis 43.11). Almonds—*Amygdalus communis*—and the almond tree played a significant role in the life of the Israelites.

Almond trees were found throughout Palestine, Syria and in the Negeb, which suggests that the trees also grew in the area around Mount Sinai—a mountain of healing and of special concern to Israel. Israel adopted the almond tree and its branches as a model for the lampstand (Exodus 25.33, 34; 37.19, 20). During the era of the Maccabees, the Israelites placed the almond design on the shekel. Within the rabbinical community and subsequently for the people, the almond stood as a powerful metaphor of the life of the Jewish people. The gnarled trees flowered and thrived despite rocky soil and goats, which chewed on the trees. The resilient tree represented the growth and endurance of the Jewish people. The bitter almond spoke of their days of slavery and displacement.

In their daily lives, the people used almond as a food and for oil. Along with olive oil, almond oil was the favored oil for burning in ceremonial lamps and for anointing.

Almond has a history of being a religious herb. The oil was used in incense. Aaron's rod, indicating his leadership and the special status of the tribe of Levi, sprouted as an almond tree.

In parts of the known world, some believed that eating five to seven almonds before drinking was helpful in preventing intoxication. A nutritious demulcent was made with an ounce of almond in a quart of water. Hippocrates used almonds in his simples. Galen, a 2nd century scholar-physician, is credited with creating a cold cream nearly 2000 years ago, which used almonds, rosebuds and olive oil. Other ancient uses for almond include fighting coughs and inflammation of the coli, and helping with headaches.

Amygdalus communis is also the almond of use today.

- In a vegetable oil base, almond essential oil is used for massage.
- Almond oil has been used for centuries all over the world as an ingredient in love potions.
- The sweet almond tree is used to produce a fixed oil through cold processing. (The essential oil from the bitter almond generally is not used in aromatherapy because of the risk of prussic acid forming during distillation.)
- Unrefined almond oil is used in laxative preparations and is effective in reducing blood cholesterol.
- Almond makes an excellent emollient that nourishes dry skin. It helps soothe inflammation and is beneficial in relieving the itching caused by eczema, psoriasis, dermatitis and all cases of dry, scaly skin.

Almond in Scripture

Genesis 30.37: fresh rods of poplar and almond. These were among the choicest fruits of the land.

Genesis 43.11: a little balm and a little honey, gum, myrrh…almonds. Suggested for taking to Egypt as a gift when purchasing corn. Because almonds were among the choicest fruits of the land, this was a most appropriate gift.

Exodus 25.32-36; 37.19-20: cups made like almonds with capitals and flowers on the golden lampstands of the Tabernacle. Almond was used as a decorative symbol, reflecting the life of the Israelites.

Numbers 17.8: the rod of Aaron had sprouted…bore ripe almonds. As a sign of Aaron's special position, almonds sealed his authority.

Ecclesiastes 12.5: the almond tree blossoms. The almond blossoms symbolize the white hair of the aged.

Jeremiah 1.11: "I see a rod of almond." This is actually a play on words. Almond in Hebrew is *shaqedh*, while the Hebrew word for watch or wake is *shoqedh*. The almond tree is the earliest to "wake" in the spring.

Aloe

The aloe of Biblical times is very different from the aloe plant found in homes today. It is thought that the aloe of the Old Testament is *Aquillaria agallocha*, a wood that was highly esteemed. The soft, fragrant inner wood was molded and shaped as a setting for precious stones. The decaying heartwood was treated with a resin and then used as a base for incense.

The aloe of the New Testament is a substance derived from leaves that were dissolved in water and added to sweet smelling incense for purifying bodies of the departed. Aloe juice was a purgative well known among the ancients.

John 19.39 records a mixture of myrrh and aloes used by Nicodemus to embalm the body of Jesus. Some botanists believe this aloe to be *Aloe succotrina*, which is a bitter, malodorous purgative medicine used for embalming. Overall, aloe was known only as an aromatic substance and not as a tree in the Holy Lands.

Aloe barbadensis is the aloe commonly known and used today. It has uses similar to the aloe of the Biblical days, even though they are not the same aloe.

- Today, aloe is used in incense burning and for embalming, as it was in Biblical times.
- Reflective of the tradition of John 19.39, some people plant aloe upon graves of loved ones to bring peace until the day of resurrection.
- Aloe is a tremendous healing agent for cuts, inflammations and burns.
- Aloe is a good carrying oil for essential oils.

- Aloe is one of the safest and best, warm and stimulating purgatives.
- In cosmetics, aloe is used as an emollient and is good for any skin problem.

Aloe in Scripture

Numbers 24.6: planted with cedars, an oracle. This reference is probably to an oak tree.
Psalm 45.8: aloes with myrrh. It was used as a fragrance.
Proverbs 7.17: aloes with myrrh. This refers to perfume, perhaps from the lign aloe or eaglewood tree of India.
Song of Solomon 4.14: aloes with myrrh.

(The preceding three references are most likely the *Aquillaria agallocha*, a type of wood.)

John 19.39: this is probably the *Aloe succotrina*. Scholars are not absolutely certain; however, it *is* different from the aloes of the Old Testament.

Apple

Tradition tells us that Eve gave Adam an apple to eat, and that simple act brought about the downfall of humanity. Artists over the centuries have depicted that scene with an apple-like fruit. Scripture simply states that Adam and Eve were not to eat of the "fruit of the tree of the knowledge of good and evil." In the RSV, apple or apples appear 10 times but none of those verses is in Genesis. Even though from a linguistic perspective *apple* is the preferred translation in these instances, common thought doubts that apple as mentioned in the scripture is apple as we understand it today. There is an absence of apple trees in the Biblical lands today except in remote areas, and those trees and their fruit are of poor quality. Possibilities as to what the apple of scripture might have been are: apricot, citron, orange or quince. The apricot and the orange are still important fruits in Bible lands today. Citron is used in preserves or is candied. Quince is the only one of the suggested possibilities that is an indigenous fruit. In light of these possibilities, apricot best fits the variety of descriptions, yet the apricot is native to China and came to the Holy Lands and the Western world no earlier than the first century B.C. What seems to have happened is that translators simply used the name of the fruit most familiar to themselves. Another thought is that throughout time the apple has been viewed as attractive, delicious and seductive; such imagery lends itself to the use of the apple in the "fall" story.

In five situations, we encounter the phrase "apple of his/your eye." This is actually an English idiom, meaning "pupil of the eye." Hence, the implication is that this is something very precious. For the Greeks, the apple was seen as a source of wisdom.

Whatever "apple" was in Biblical times, we understand that it is not the same as what we call "apple" today, though people of the Bible used their "apple" and its juice as we do today—for nutritional purposes.

- Additionally, we use apples to help neutralize acid products of gout and indigestion and, in general, to help digest other foods.
- Fresh apple pulp is used to make facial masks, hand creams, and pomades.
- Apple cider diluted with water is a natural astringent.

Apple in Scripture

The four references in which we encounter "apple of his/your eye" and thus the inference to something precious are these:

Deuteronomy 32.10: the song of Moses, reminding God that the Israelites wandering in the wilderness were precious to God.
Psalm 17.8: part of a prayer for deliverance in which the psalmist asks God to see him as precious.
Proverbs 7.2: describes wisdom as a safeguard against adultery, if one keeps wisdom as a precious thing.
Zechariah 2.8: an appeal to the exiles from the prophet to remember that they are precious to God.

Other references:

Proverbs 25.11: "A word fitly spoken is like apples of gold." This suggests that "apple" might actually be apricot, because the apricots of that area were golden in color.
Song of Solomon 2.3, 5: "As the apple tree is special so is the love special, and the maiden longs for love when the time is ripe."
Song of Solomon 7.8: descriptive imagery.
Song of Solomon 8.5: descriptive of location.
Joel 1.12: "All the trees of the field are withered." This was an effect of the locust plague and, for Joel, a sign of God's judgment upon a wayward people.

Balm

To speak of balm as used in the Bible lands among the people is to acknowledge that it had a widespread therapeutic use; it is also to acknowledge that the true identity of that balm has never been established. Some have suggested that it is *Balsamodendron opobalsamum*, which was native to Arabia and Abyssinia. This balm was used for cosmetics and embalming. Winifred Walker, author of *All the Plants of the Bible*, argues for false balm of Gilead as a gum resin that came from the bark of an evergreen shrub (*Balanites aegyptiaca*), which until the 17th century was an ingredient in many medicines. Sixteenth century Swiss physician and alchemist, Paracelsus, believed that balm would "revivify" a person.

Today's balm is generally recognized as *Melissa officinalis*:

- It is a veritable cornucopia for aromatherapy.
- Balm is used as an antiseptic, antispasmodic, anti-viral and anti-inflammatory medication.
- Balm has a calming or sedative effect. It is used as a carminative, diaphoretic to ease stomach cramps and nausea.
- Balm also eases the pain of fever and headache.
- It promotes perspiration.
- Balm works on insomnia.
- It is good for skin, especially when used in a bath.
- It is an excellent surgical dressing.
- Use of balm can help promote spiritual growth, help with bereavement, depression and grief. Balm brings a feeling of peace to individuals.

Note: The majority of *melissa* oils on the market today are synthetic.

Balm in Scripture

Balm occurs six times. Three of the references speak of balm for its commercial or trade value:

Genesis 37.25: the Joseph story. A caravan passes through the area with camels bearing gum, balm and myrrh. A curious image can be suggested as the caravan deals in balm, a healing agent, but Jacob's family is about to be torn asunder as the brothers sell their brother, Joseph, to the caravan traders. Ironically, years later one of the gifts that Jacob has his sons take to the "foreign" ruler (who happens to be Joseph) is balm.
Genesis 43.11: Jacob charges his sons to go to Egypt and to take a present, including a little balm.
Ezekiel 27.17: A lamentation over Tyre, exchanging merchandise which included balm.

The best known reference of balm in scripture is found in Jeremiah, where the prophet speaks of the balm of Gilead. The three references in Jeremiah declare that no healing is going to occur, even though healing is sorely needed:

Jeremiah 8.22: "Is there no balm in Gilead?" A lament over Judah. The prophet expressed concern about the wholeness of the people. There are no physicians; how can people expect to become well?
Jeremiah 46.11: oracles against foreign nations. Go up to Gilead and take balm; work for healing.
Jeremiah 51.8: speaks of God's judgment against Babylon. The verse is somewhat "tongue in cheek," for Babylon's case is hopeless.

Balsam

Commiphora opobalsamum is also called *Balsamodendron opobalsamum*. Some scholars offer this plant as a possibility for what was known and referred to in the scripture as balm. The problem is that this plant never grew around Jerusalem but only in South Arabia. Another thought is that the balsam was *Populus euphratica* and is the balsam tree that is referred to in the RSV. The difficulty here is that there is no evidence that the relevant verses actually refer to any plant.

The ancient historian, Josephus, recorded that balsam came to Judea from Arabia as one of the gifts that the Queen of Sheba brought to Solomon. Legend suggests that Solomon then had balsam cultivated on Mount Gilead.

Susanne Fischer-Rizzi writes in *The Complete Incense Book* that there is a tree called Mecca, or "Balm of Gilead," which had a yellow fragrant seed that the people boiled and pressed into a wax-like substance for incense burning. This tree grew mainly in the forests of Gilead and the mountains around Mecca. Legend says that Mary Magdalene's father owned a balsam forest and he was under orders from the king to produce consecrated oil. Both the oil used for consecration and the frankincense used in the Temple contained balsam.

Cooley, writing in 1892, stated that balsam was originally any strong-scented oleo-resinous vegetable juice or exudation about the fluidity of treacle. It was supposed to possess medicinal virtues.

Whatever the balsam was, it was an important and valued commodity for commerce. People used balsam for perfumery, for embalming and for treating diseases of the urinary tract.

Given the uncertainty from scripture as to what balsam actually referred to in those days, a reliable comparison to balsam today cannot be offered.

- There is *Graphalium polycephalum, Populus nigra Salicaceae* and *Balsamodendron gileandensis.* These are used in incense and as medicines for rheumatism, fever, hemorrhoids and bladder diseases.

Balsam in Scripture

II Samuel 5.23, 24: balsam tree, a place to stand, "hear the sound of marching in the tops of the trees." The tree is probably a *mastic terebinth,* which is more like a bush than a tree. This must have been a particularly prominent bush. Hans Wilhelm Hertzberg comments that the "steps" of the Lord, which is the sign for the attack, will have been seen in the distinct waving movements in the tops of the trees. Another scholar argues that mulberry is the better translation for the word "baka." There was a belief that trees served as abodes of divine beings and as media of divination and revelation. This was deeply rooted in early Semitic thought.

II Chronicles 14.14-15: same as previous reference

Bdellium

What is bdellium, really? Is it a precious stone, a pearl, a gum, a resin? The word's origin and use suggest that bdellium is a gum. Its use in Genesis suggests that bdellium is a stone. In the book of Numbers, the use suggests a pearl, as it describes manna that comes as "white hoarfrost." The LXX understands it as a rock crystal.

A 16th century English herbalist wrote of a tree that grew in Havilah (see Genesis 2.11ff.), a territory east of Persia, which gave off an aromatic gum known as bdellium. The gum oozed from the tree, hardened, became waxy and transparent, and looked like a pearl. Women carried these in little pouches to use as perfume.

Bdellium today is recognized as inferior myrrh and probably a product of one of several species of *Commiphora* (American) or *Balsamodendron* (English).

- It has been used to battle leprosy and rheumatism.

Bdellium in Scripture

Genesis 2.12: description of land. Bdellium and onyx stone are there.
Numbers 11.7: Israel's murmuring in the wilderness about food. Manna looks like bdellium.

Calamus

Choice of scripture translation surfaces here. Exodus 30.23 in the KJV refers to calamus; the RSV translates it as "sweet cane." In Jeremiah 6.20 and Isaiah 43.24, both the RSV and KJV speak of sweet cane, which some scholars suggest is calamus. The plant apparently comes from the genus *Cymbopogon*, and scholars are uncertain as to exactly which species this calamus might be. What is known is that it was a product of trade and made from an aromatic reed or grass, which was most likely imported from India.

Cymbopogon schoenanthus has been found in old Egyptian tombs. Some researchers believe this to be one of the ingredients of the "sacred perfume" of the ancient Egyptians. Kyphi or Cyphi was a composition perfume welcome to the gods. Combined with cinnamon, calamus was used as a salve by the Egyptians throughout antiquity. As an incense mixture with cedar and myrtle, it was used as a nerve tonic.

Today's calamus is *Acorus calamus* of the *Araceae* family.

- It is used as an anticonvulsant, antiseptic, antibacterial, expectorant and stimulant.
- This calamus helps with exhaustion, loss of appetite, and indigestion.
- Calamus works as a part of inhalation therapy for nerves, headache and hypochondria.
- Small bits of calamus may be chewed to clear the voice and strengthen the throat.
- Some potpourris contain calamus.

Calamus in Scripture

Song of Solomon 4.14: from a section that speaks of youth. This verse provides a rich imagery of luxury and fertility.
Ezekiel 27.19: a product of trade.

Cassia

Cinnamomum cassia or, simply, cassia, is the aromatic bark of an oriental tree. There is a reference to cassia wood in the Qumran Cave scroll. Cassia was probably imported to Palestine from South Arabia, a famous trade center of drugs, incense and spices during Biblical times. It was a primary article of commerce. In ancient Babylonia, the shekel was a measurement of weight, equivalent to the weight of a half-ounce of cassia. Cassia was part of the holy anointing oil.

Cinnamomum cassia is often substituted today for *Cinnamomum zeylanicum*.

- It is used in cooking and in incense. (Cassia is the "cinnamon" that one usually purchases in the market place, since *Cinnamomum zeylanicum* is very costly and rare.)
- Cassia acts as a stomachic, carminative and is mildly astringent as a decoction.
- The oil stimulates the pancreas and also acts as a germicide.
- Most cola-type drinks contain cassia.
- Cassia is also found in some potpourris.

Cassia in Scripture

Exodus 30.24: The passage in which this verse appears, describes the holy oil. Cassia is a part of that oil.

Psalm 45.8: This psalm is an ode for a royal marriage. The royal bridegroom's robes are fragrant.

Ezekiel 27.19: Cassia is mentioned as an item for barter or merchandise.

Cedar

The RSV is replete with references to cedar, cedars and cedarwood. This cedar is most likely *Cedrus Libani*. The word cedar in Hebrew comes from an old Arabian derivation meaning "a firmly rooted, strong tree." The cedar was indeed a mighty, long-living tree, which grew to 100 feet or so in height and could have a trunk with a diameter of six to nine feet. It never grew in Palestine. Cedar was used for pillars, support beams, roofing, paneling, ceilings in buildings and for ship masts. Cedar became a symbol or metaphor of strength, splendor, grandeur, majesty, might or glory. The Arabs called cedars, "trees of the Lord." When appearing in the scripture, cedar generally represents one of the preceding characteristics or else is spoken of as a building material.

The cedarwood that is mentioned in the purification of homes and lepers was probably *Pinus halepensis* or *Juniperus phoenicea*. Legend has it that when King Solomon fathered a son, he would plant a cedar tree. When he fathered a daughter, Solomon would plant a pine. At the time of the child's marriage, his or her tree was cut down and used to make the nuptial bed. The symbolism was that of purity, constancy and incorruptibility.

Cedar is possibly the oldest perfume material known. Its distillate of oil probably began 5,500 years ago.

Cedrus atlantica resembles *Cedrus libani*, which is now a protected species.

- Some suggest that *Cedrus atlantica* is not known for any unique medicinal properties but for its ability to gently, but persistently, stimulate circulation and metabolism.

- It is useful as an antibacterial, antiseptic, stimulant, cicatrisant, antispasmodic, emmenagogue, expectorant and anticatarrhal.
- This particular cedar is not good for timber purposes.

Cedars and Cedarwood in Scripture

Numbers 24.6: aloes planted like cedar trees. This refers to construction and strength.

Judges 9.15: part of an absurd fable—the worthless and insignificant can sometimes fell the noble and mighty.

II Samuel 5.11: construction.

II Samuel 7.2,7: construction.

I Kings 4.33: discussion of Solomon's wisdom. He even knows about cedar trees.

I Kings 5.6, 8, 10: Hiram will meet Solomon's needs for cedar in the building of the temple.

I Kings 6.9, 10, 15, 16, 18, 20, 36: temple construction. Cedar used for strength and fragrance.

I Kings 7.2, 3, 7, 11, 12: House of Forest, Hall of Throne—two buildings south of the palace court, which was itself south of the temple court. Cedar was the primary building material.

I Kings 9.11: discussion of how Solomon paid Hiram for the supply of cedar.

I Kings 10.27: metaphor for how common or plentiful cedar had become in Jerusalem under Solomon.

II Kings 14.9: a parable. What happens when a little thistle sets itself up to being equal to a cedar?

II Kings 19.23: part of a battle dialogue. That which seems strong, or that can fell the strong, may still be overcome by the Lord.

I Chronicles 14.1: Hiram sends cedar to Solomon.

I Chronicles 17.1, 6: similar to II Samuel 7.

I Chronicles 22.4: cedar timber without number.

II Chronicles 1.15: parallels I Kings 10.26.

II Chronicles 2.3, 8: building the temple. Send more cedar.

II Chronicle 9.27: similar to II Chronicles 1.15.

II Chronicles 25.18: parallels II Kings 14.9.

Ezra 3.7: work begins on the rebuilding of the temple.
Job 40.17: cedar used to describe characteristics of Behemoth.
Psalm 29.5: voice of God breaks cedars. Shows strength.
Psalm 37.35: wicked person described as towering like Lebanon cedar. "The bigger they are, the harder they fall."
Psalm 80.10: Israel's resolute confidence in God. Mighty cedars, mighty God.
Psalm 92.12: The righteous grow like cedar—strong, majestic.
Psalm 104.16: hymn to God, recalling God's creative power.
Psalm 148.9: a summon to earth to come praise. "Let heaven and earth praise God."
Song of Solomon 1.17: The beams of the house are cedar. Shows splendor, strength.
Song of Solomon 5.15: description of the youth. Lebanon is known for its beauty, fertility and cedars.
Song of Solomon 8.9: confusing passage in its intended imagery, perhaps an imagery of chastity.
Isaiah 2.13: features that have awed men throughout time—height and strength.
Isaiah 9.10: a word of judgment. People are filled with pride and wickedness, thinking they can overcome adversaries and continue to stand, even as the cedars stand.
Isaiah 14.8: The rule of the tyrant has been broken by God, and the earth rejoices.
Isaiah 37.24: sets forth impending doom of Assyrian King.
Isaiah 41.19: an interlude of comfort and assurance. Symbol of stability, sense of majesty.
Isaiah 44.14: part of a parody on the making of idols.
Jeremiah 22.7, 23: parts of oracles of destruction describing how acute the destruction/downfall will be.
Jeremiah 22.14, 15: oracle against Jehoiakim. Signs and symbols do not necessarily a strong king make.
Ezekiel 17.3, 22, 23: an allegory of two eagles and a cedar—cedar as part of symbolism.
Ezekiel 27.5: strong ship of Tyre made with cedar.

Ezekiel 31.3, 8: allegory with Egypt as the great cedar.
Amos 2.9: God can destroy, regardless of how big or strong a people believe themselves to be.
Zephaniah 2.14: part of a warning issued to Assyria.
Zechariah 11.1, 2: fall of tyrants. Even those who see themselves as strong or mighty as cedar can be felled by God.

The following two references are to *Cedarwood*, which the above discussion cited as being different from cedar.

Leviticus 14.4, 6, 49, 51, 52: the cleansing of leprosy in a person and in a house.
Numbers 19.6: purification rites.

Cedarwood was used by the Levites during sacrifices and also is associated with hyssop and scarlet.

Cinnamon

Cinnamomum zeylanicum of the family *Lauraceae* spans the centuries. It is the fine quality, true cinnamon of Biblical times and today. It comes from the fragrant bark of an oriental tree and is highly valued as a spice. Actually, cinnamon was seen as more than a "mere spice" in Biblical times. It was used to prepare incense and holy oils for various religious rites, medicines and perfumes. Cinnamon also found use in the embalming process. Some folks believed cinnamon to be an aphrodisiac. It was a valuable trade item as well.

- Today, cinnamon continues to find use in incense, as an aromatic, and in food.
- Cinnamon is placed in some hair dye.
- Cinnamon in its various forms is used as an antiemetic, antiseptic, astringent, stimulant, antiviral, antibacterial, disinfectant, antispasmodic, antifungal and carminative.
- Cinnamon works favorably upon digestive disorders. It is a good general tonic for the reproductive system.
- Some still use cinnamon as an aphrodisiac.
- Cinnamon can be irritating on mucous surfaces and sensitive skin and should not be used during pregnancy or with young children.

Cinnamon in Scripture
Exodus 30.23: part of the recipe for the holy anointing oil.
Proverbs 7.17: The context suggests its use as an aphrodisiac, part of a long treatise advising against being caught up in illicit love. Wisdom is the better pursuit.
Song of Solomon 4.14: part of the extended description of love.

Revelation 18.13: part of a dirge over the fallen city. The desolation is so complete that commercial trade and merchandising no longer take place. Cinnamon is one of the items no longer available.

Coriander

Coriandrum sativum is the coriander of Biblical times and of today as well. However, there is a difficulty. The two references to coriander are in the Pentateuch, where they are used to describe manna. The description speaks of the white flakes of manna, like coriander seed, but coriander seeds are brown! Over the centuries, two possible explanations have surfaced: Perhaps manna resembles coriander seed in the size and shape of the seeds. Perhaps the comparison actually refers to the blossom or flower of the coriander and not to the seeds.

Records indicate that coriander was used for culinary and medicinal purposes as early as 1550 B.C. Apparently, coriander seeds were used in much the same way as we use poppy, caraway and sesame seeds today. Coriander seeds were part of Kyphi recipes. The incense was used to ease severe tension, depression and chronic headache pain.

- In addition to wide use in the food industry today, coriander finds use as a carminative, analgesic, antibacterial, and antispasmodic.
- Coriander is a stomachic and promotes digestion.
- It is also used as an anti-inflammatory.
- As a massage oil, coriander is rubbed on the temples to help with migraine headaches.
- Coriander is an aromatic stimulant.
- Coriander has been described as an herb of protection, associated with peace.
- If one is feeling aggressive, one may find coriander to be settling.
- Conversely, coriander can create a mild feeling of euphoria. It

can be uplifting and energizing.

Coriander in Scripture

Exodus 16.31: God provides quail and manna, and manna is described in relation to coriander. The difficulty or challenge of this description is discussed above. **Numbers 11.7:** compares manna to coriander, then states that manna is like bdellium in appearance.

"Scholars are generally agreed that manna is the sweet, sticky exudation of the *Tamarix gallica*, which come out at night and fall to the ground. Like small pieces of wax before the sun gets up (a coriander seed is about the size of a peppercorn), they melt in the daytime heat. Fresh supplies come each night in June and July, and are used by Arabs for pouring or spreading on bread. The color is yellowish like bdellium, a resinous gum."

—The Interpreter's Bible, vol. 2, p. 195.

Cucumber

Scholars rather much agree that the cucumber mentioned in scripture is a vegetable or fruit of the genus *Cucumis*. Word study of the Hebrew and Greek, beginning with the LXX, suggests *Cucumis sativus* or *Cucumis chate*. It is believed to be the common cucumber. Difficulty exists in that there is no evidence that cucumbers grew in Egypt in Biblical times. Evidence or indications do exist for the growth and cultivation of three other, similar vegetables/fruits: *Cucumis melo, Cucumis chate*, and *Lagenaria leucantha. Cucumis melo* is known to us as muskmelon, and this type of fruit (tasty as it is) would be missed by a people accustomed to eating it. *Lagenaria leucanth* was very much present in Biblical times.

Whatever the cucumber was, we do understand it to have been a delicacy (in taste, not in cost) and always desired by the people. Because of its apparent abundance, the cucumber was an important food for the poor. However, people of all status and income found the cucumber to be a gratifying food, for in the hot climate cucumber was refreshing and cooling.

Once folks became accustomed to eating cucumber, life without cucumber was unthinkable. Apparently, guards protected cucumber fields just as they protected vineyards and olive orchards. One of the arguments for cucumber's being muskmelon is that lodges were put in melon fields and not in cucumber fields.

Cucumis sativus is the common cucumber in our markets.

- Some describe cucumber as a visionary herb that brings a sense of peace to the soul, a sense of calm to one's well being.
- The green rind of the cucumber placed across one's closed eyelids

brings the individual in closer touch with one's subconscious.
- Cucumber is most widely used in herbal cosmetics. It is the naturalist beautician's panacea.
- Cucumber is found in creams, lotions, sunburn preparations, soaps and masks and in ointments for cutaneous eruptions and irritated skin.
- Cucumber works on smoothing away wrinkles and blemishes and is used in combination with other herbs and materials in aftershaves and perfumes.

Cucumber/Cucumbers in Scripture

Numbers 11.5: Israelites murmur in the wilderness over food that they missed. Melon also is mentioned in this listing, so clearly there is a difference between cucumber and melon.
Isaiah 1.8: "… like a lodge in a cucumber field." This verse is part of an extended passage that is an oracle against rebellious Judah. As mentioned in the text above, the problem with this verse is that the melon fields had lodges in them, not cucumber fields (see also melon).
Jeremiah 10.5: "Idols are like scarecrows in a cucumber field." This is an image of worthlessness. A scarecrow is not needed in a cucumber field.

Cummin (Biblical)
or Cumin (Modern day)

Cuminum cyminum has been cultivated in the Mediterranean area since about 1300 B.C. Cummin was used extensively in Biblical times, but it is not so common in the area today. Cummin was used as a condiment, for seasoning foods. It was mixed with bread or added to meat. Cummin was a powerful aromatic seed. Its medicinal properties were known to the ancients, who took ground cummin seed medicinally with bread, water and/or wine, using it as a stimulant, antispasmodic and carminative.

- *Cuminum cyminum* or "cumin" is used today for its calming, stupefying effects.
- It continues to see use as a strong anti-spasmodic, a digestive stimulant and a carminative.
- Cumin is used in massage oil for poor circulation and for lymphatic congestion.
- Cumin oil is used in the food industry.
- Some people use cumin in rituals to protect their homes and to provide internal protection.
- There is some use of cumin in perfumery.

Cumin in Scripture
Isaiah 28.25, 27: "Does he not scatter dill and sow cumin?" This is part of a parable of the farmer. The loving kindness of God is extended to Israel, just as God extended concern to the sowing and harvesting of even the smallest of seeds.

Matthew 23.23: "Tithe dill, mint, cumin." Religious leaders had concern for the smallest details of the law but not necessarily for the health and well being of individuals, if such a concern posed a risk to maintaining and/or obeying the law.

Cypress

The earliest occurrence of the word cypress is found on a 14th century B.C. tablet at Ugaret. Scholars have difficulty defining specifically what cypress refers to in the scripture. The KJV uses "box tree" in some verses. The American translation refers to "larch," and occasionally the RSV translates the word as "pine." Box tree is a problematic translation because the box tree was neither native to, nor grown in, Palestine. The cypress tree is native to Palestine and grows wild in Gilead and Edom. Cypress was used in ornamental settings as well as for windbreaks. Because of its durability, cypress found tremendous use in construction: rafters, joists, decks of ships, wine presses. Apocryphal writings suggest that cypress grew on Mount Hermon.

Over the centuries, cypress became a holy tree, a symbol of long life. It was used in incense burning to promote healing, especially for the respiratory tract. People believed that using cypress incense helped them get a "fresh start," to set goals and to resolve old grief and disappointments.

The cypress of scripture was *Cupressus sempervirens*, which is the same cypress used today in aromatherapy.

- Cypress is an antibacterial, anti-infectious, antispasmodic, antisudorific, astringent, and diuretic.
- Cypress has a general hygienic effect on urinary tract infections as well as on infections of the throat, nose or bronchi in early stages.
- Cypress can be inhaled dry during asthma attacks.
- As part of a bath or in massage oil, cypress relieves aching

muscles, abdominal cramps and menstrual cramps.
- In emotional healing, cypress works on confusion, depression and exhaustion.

Cypress/Cypresses in Scripture

I Kings 5.8, 10: Hiram supplies Solomon with all the cedar and cypress that he needs.

I Kings 6.15, 34: use of cypress in construction of part of the Temple floor and two doors.

I Kings 9.11: Hiram supplied Solomon with cypress.

II Kings 19.23: image of destruction and judgment. The cypress, which is strong and sturdy, is easily cut down.

II Chronicles 2.8: Solomon prepares to build temple and orders cypress.

II Chronicles 3.5: The nave of the Temple is covered with cypress.

Isaiah 14.8: Israel returns from exile. Even the trees that have been plundered by oppressive kings for their building projects rejoice, because the trees are no longer threatened.

Isaiah 37.24: Isaiah challenges Sennacherib and Sennacherib's power against the real power of God.

Isaiah 41.19: a description of the restoration of the people and the land. Cypress will be planted. This is one passage in which scholars are quite certain that *Cupressus sempervirens* is the tree.

Isaiah 55.13: an image of a new Exodus into a new Eden-like land. Cypress is evocative of long life and durability.

Isaiah 60.13: similar to I Kings 5.8, 10 in construction image. Also lifts up the theme of long life and durability. Similar to Isaiah 41.19, in that *Cupressus sempervirens* is clearly the tree mentioned.

Ezekiel 27.6: "Of oaks of Bashan they made your oars; they made your deck of pines from the coasts of Cyprus, inlaid with ivory" (RSV). Pine is used instead of cypress; however, the ancient language suggests that it is the same *Cupressus sempervirens* translated as cypress elsewhere in the RSV.

Hosea 14.8: "I am like an evergreen cypress." God guides and sustains Israel.

Zechariah 11.2: the fall of tyrants. Even those who believe themselves to be impregnable can be, and are, defeated and dethroned by God.

Dill

In the RSV, dill is mentioned twice: once in the Old Testament and once in the New Testament. Research suggests that each refers to a different plant. The Old Testament dill was probably *Nigella sativa*, also called the nutmeg flower but not related to the nutmeg tree. In the New Testament, dill is *Anethum graveolens*, which is what we know as dill in modern times. A similar history applies to dill as was noted for apple. The word that is translated dill in the RSV is translated "anise" or "black cumin" in other versions. The difference appears to depend upon the writer. Noted Bible translator John Wicklif erroneously rendered the Greek word as anise in his 1380 translation and the error has been continued over the centuries in other versions and publications.

What is known is that dill is a kind of a seed used as a condiment or a seasoning. In centuries past dill saw use as a flavoring, carminative, breath freshener, stimulant, aromatic, stomachic and as a healing wash for skin conditions. Dill was used to "draw down the milk" of nursing mothers; and, as a decoction, dill was good for women with "womb griefs."

Dill continues with many of the same uses today:

- It is used as a carminative, stimulant, aromatic and stomachic.
- It also sees use as a digestive aid, a cure for hiccoughs and relief from stomach gas; it stimulates the secretion of gastric juices.
- Dill serves as an anti-spasmodic and an anti-catarrhal.
- It is a good fixative for most medicines for children.
- Some describe dill as an herb of protection and blessing.

Dill in Scripture

Isaiah 28.25, 27: dill and cummin, the parable of the farmer. (See same scripture reference under cumin.) Most likely, the plant intended was the nutmeg flower or black cumin.

Matthew 23.23: "You tithe mint...dill." Real dill. (See same scripture reference under cumin.)

Fig/Figs

The *Ficus carica* or fig is the first fruit mentioned in the Bible: Adam and Eve sewed fig leaves together to create clothing. The fig is one of seven plants promised by God for the Hebrews when they reached the Promised Land (wheat, barley, grapes or vine, figs, honey or date palm and olive). In scripture, the fig is a symbol of prosperity and peace. In some of the Biblical narratives, it is helpful to know that Bethphage means house or place of unripe figs; Bethany means house of figs.

The fig held great importance in the life of Israel. The fig tree offered heavy shade and relief from the hot sun. It also provided delicious fruit, with the fruit having different uses in its various stages of growing and ripening. The tree and vine symbolized freedom and prosperity. Figs were used to make cakes, wine and a sweetener. The best figs were dried individually; the second best figs were strung together and dried. Ordinary figs were pressed into cakes. People wove fig leaves into baskets, dishes and umbrellas. Figs served as a laxative and/or a tonic. Poultices were made to treat infections, tumors and boils. In ancient mythology, figs were used in religious ceremonies and also as an aphrodisiac.

- Today we continue to use figs as a food and as a laxative.
- We still make poultices to treat swelling, sores or dental abrasions.
- Figs also are used as a mild purgative, to soothe coughs, and as a mild expectorant.
- A coffee substitute, an emollient and a cleansing mask are other uses.

Fig/Figs in Scripture

The majority of scriptural references to the fig or figs are metaphorical.

Genesis 3.7: Adam and Eve sewed fig leaves together; first fruit mentioned in the Bible.

Numbers 13.23: territory "surveyed" by spies; fig trees are in the land. This implies that this is a good land.

Numbers 20.5: Israelites complain because area in which they find themselves does not have figs, and figs are an essential part of their life.

Deuteronomy 8.8: God has carried, and cared for, the people through the wilderness, bringing them now to a bountiful land that includes figs; people should remember the journey and not become filled with self pride.

Judges 9.10, 11: part of a fable reflecting on the character of a leader (Abimelech).

I Samuel 25.18: how David obtained his second wife, Abigail. She made pressed figs, which in those times were also used as poultices.

I Samuel 30.12: figs as food.

I Kings 4.25: symbolism of peace and prosperity in Solomon's organization of the kingdom. Every man will have a vine and fig tree.

II Kings 18.31: a metaphor for peace, but there will be no peace.

II Kings 20.7: Hezekiah's illness and recovery; bring a cake of figs. Food or perhaps poultice.

I Chronicles 12.40: part of a story of David's accomplishments. figs symbolize food, peace and prosperity.

Nehemiah 13.15: a recounting of Sabbath-breaking; figs being harvested.

Psalm 105.33: story of God's great deeds on behalf of God's people.

Proverbs 27.18: "He who tends a fig tree will eat its fruit." A metaphor for hard work and prosperity.

Song of Solomon 2.13: lover comes to summon bride. The fig tree puts forth its figs—spring, green fruit. A metaphor for life and hope.

Isaiah 28.4: oracles concerning Judah and Ephraim; will be like a first ripe fig before summer. Early fruit, often the best fruit.
Isaiah 34.4: terrible end of God's enemies. As leaves fall; like leaves falling from the fig tree (stars as fruit on heavenly tree and stars will fall as leaves fall from tree) A metaphor for end of peace and prosperity.
Isaiah 36.16: speech intended to demoralize Jerusalem's defenders. Every one his own fig tree. A metaphor for peace.
Isaiah 38.21: Hezekiah's illness and recovery. Let them take a cake of figs and apply it to the boil. A poultice.
Jeremiah 5.17: judgment for corruption. They shall eat up your vines and your fig trees. Pending doom.
Jeremiah 8.13: Judah will be destroyed. No grapes on the vine, nor figs on the fig tree. Pending doom.
Jeremiah 24.1, 2, 3, 5, 8: vision of baskets of figs, good and bad figs. A metaphor for life and death, peace and prosperity or destruction and doom.
Jeremiah 29.17: Jeremiah's letter to Babylon. "And I will make them like vile figs." Doom.
Ezekiel 27.17: lamentation over Tyre. Exchanged for your merchandise wheat, olives and early figs. Doom.
Hosea 2.12: Israel will suffer public shame. Lay waste her vines and her fig trees. Doom.
Hosea 9.10: Israel rejects God and will be punished. Like the first fig on the fig tree. Doom.
Joel 1.7, 12: locust plague. It has laid waste my vines and splintered my fig tree. Pending doom.
Joel 2.22: locust plague. The tree bears its fruit, the fig tree. Peace and prosperity.
Amos 4.9: Israel's excesses and vain piety. Your fig trees and your olive trees the locust devoured. Doom.
Amos 8.1-2: basket of summer fruit believed to be over ripe figs. *Gayits* is wordplay on *qets*, which means "end."
Micah 4.4: prophecy of future restoration. "They shall sit…under his vine and under his fig tree." Peace and prosperity, feeling of

security.

Micah 7.1: lament. No first ripe fig, which my soul desires. Looking for honest person, which prophet cannot find. Sense of doom.

Nahum 3.12: sack of Nineveh. All your fortresses are like fig trees with first ripe figs, which are quickly gone. Pending doom.

Habakkuk 3.17: Habakkuk's prayer. Though the fig trees do not blossom—hope for peace and prosperity.

Haggai 2.19: temple foundation laid; God blesses. "Do the vine, the fig tree, the pomegranate still bear nothing?" Peace and prosperity.

Zechariah 3.10: under the vine and under the fig tree. A situation of victory, release.

(In the parables in which Jesus speaks of a leafy but barren fig tree, the fruitless tree symbolizes hopelessness. It was similar to what Jesus saw in Jerusalem: lots of practice of worshiping God, but no response to Jesus' message from God. Jesus' teaching provides an omen of disaster to come upon the city.)

Matthew 7.16: Sermon on the Mount. "Are your grapes gathered from thorns, or figs from thistles?" Fruit.

Matthew 21.19, 20, 21: fig tree cursed. A choice between doom or peace and prosperity.

Matthew 24.32: end of the age. From the fig tree learn its lesson—choice between doom or peace and prosperity.

Mark 11.13, 20, 21: similar to Matthew 21 above.

Mark 13.28: similar to Matthew 24 above.

Luke 6.44: practical teaching, similar to Matthew 7 above.

Luke 13.6, 7: I have come seeking fruit on this fig tree. Peace.

Luke 21.29: similar to Mark 13 and Matthew 24.

John 1.48, 50: testimony of Jesus' first disciples. "When you were under the fig tree." Shade.

James 3.12: true wisdom. "Can a fig tree…yield olives or a grapevine figs?"

Revelation 6.13: fifth and sixth seals. "As the fig tree sheds it winter fruit." Fruit.

Frankincense

Frankincense (*Boswella carterii*) was imported into Palestine from Arabia. A quick glance at the scripture references listed below readily indicates that frankincense was an essential ingredient of the holy rituals of Israel, part of the holy incense. Frankincense could not be used for any purpose other than those outlined in the Levitical law. Incense compounded with any other recipe than that of the law could not be offered to God nor displayed in holy places. Frankincense and the bread of presence were set before the Holy of Holies. Frankincense and oil were added to cereal offerings. People were not allowed to add frankincense to sin offerings or to a cereal offering of jealousy.

Frankincense was of the finest burning resin. Along with using it in religious rituals and offerings, the people also used frankincense in protecting, cleansing, and purifying the soul and spirit. Those with leprosy sought out frankincense as an aid to healing the disease. Frankincense was used as a fumigant and was part of the embalming process. Some believed it acted as an antidote to hemlock.

For 5,000 years frankincense has held an important role in spiritual healing.

- Churches utilize frankincense because it initiates enlightenment and protects individuals from the materialistic world.
- Frankincense releases the subconscious and uplifts the spirit. Valerie Ann Worwood describes frankincense as an "adaptogenic," meaning that frankincense adapts to the person's spiritual state of being, like an old friend, lending support in a wide range of circumstances.

- In addition to the ongoing spiritual use of frankincense, frankincense is also employed as an analgesic, anti-septic, astringent, tonic, an inhalant for colds and coughs.
- Frankincense is anticatarrhal, anti-infectious, an anti-inflammatory and a cicatrizant.
- It is a relaxing antidepressant and an immunostimulant.

Frankincense in Scripture

Exodus 30.34: "Make an incense pure and holy." The "recipe" for the holy or sacred incense.

Leviticus 2.1, 2, 15, 16: cereal offering using frankincense.

Leviticus 5.11: A sin offering should not include frankincense.

Leviticus 6.15: cereal offering with frankincense.

Leviticus 24.7: bread of presence and frankincense as an offering.

Numbers 5.15: Frankincense is not to be a part of a cereal offering of jealousy.

Nehemiah 13.5, 9: frankincense as a part of offerings made by Nehemiah.

Song of Solomon 3.6: column of smoke perfumed with...frankincense. Is the smoke actually a cloud of dust stirred up by procession, or is it a cloud from profusely burning incense? This also could be a reference to the "pillar of cloud by day and pillar of fire by night" that led the Israelites. In other words, an example of a theophany (see Exodus 13.21, 22; 14.19, 24).

Song of Solomon 4.6, 14: part of an extended description of love, including nard, saffron, calamus and cinnamon.

Isaiah 43.23: The prophet speaks words of indictment from God upon the Israelites. This contrasts what people have offered to God and what God has given to the people.

Isaiah 60.6: "camels shall bring...frankincense." It is imported to the Bible lands.

Isaiah 66.3: part of a memorial offering.

Jeremiah 6.20: indication again that frankincense is imported. Also, the offering is no longer accepted because people simply made offerings in an attempt to curry God's favor and did not follow up

with appropriate behavior.
Jeremiah 17.26: part of offerings presented to God.
Matthew 2.11: one of the gifts brought by the magi. Symbolizes the spiritual nature of the infant Jesus.
Revelation 18.13: dirge over fallen city. Merchandise trade is no longer possible.

Galbanum

The galbanum of the Bible was probably *Ferula galbaniflua*, which is the galbanum of today. Galbanum is described as a giant fennel imported from Persia and India, an incense of the tabernacle. It also was one of the ingredients of the incense for the golden altar in the Holy place. Galbanum, along with myrrh, was the incense burned most often by people in their homes. With a pungent, yet pleasant, odor, it found use as a fumigant. In Asia people used galbanum as medicine and incense. Galbanum helps to extend the life of incense. The fragrance helps calm people who have nervous states or anxiety attacks. For the Romans, galbanum represented the smell of green. People used galbanum to ease the pain of toothache and to heal internal ailments.

- Today galbanum finds it primary use as a fixative in perfumery and incense.
- Galbanum is a stimulant, expectorant, antispasmodic, antiseptic and analgesic.
- It encourages calm and stability within individuals.
- For many people the sacrificial fragrance of galbanum helps shed old ideas and bring them to total surrender to the Creator.

Galbanum in Scripture

Exodus 30.34: part of the recipe for holy oil (along with frankincense).

Ecclesiasticus 24.15: essentially the same list of ingredients as in Exodus 30.34. Here the list praises the pursuit of wisdom *[Note: Ecclesiasticus is also known as Sirach]*.

Garlic

Tradition declares that 100,000 men labored for 30 years to build the pyramids and they were fed garlic daily. Garlic—*Allium sativum*—was a staple food grown in abundance in Egypt. When the Hebrew people began their journey in the Wilderness, garlic was one of the foods that they craved. They ate it cooked or raw with bread. In Islam, the suggestion is made that garlic sprung from the steps of Satan. Garlic was left as an offering in Egyptian tombs.

The ancients believed garlic to be an herb of protection. The Talmud discusses five properties of garlic consumed on the Shabbat: 1) keeps body warm, 2) increases semen, 3) brightens the face, 4) kills parasites, 5) fosters love and removes jealousy. Garlic was believed to increase virility, to battle intestinal infections and respiratory ailments. It was also used for treatment of snakebites. Paterson, in *A Fountain of Gardens: Plants and Herbs of the Bible*, suggests that the healing power and qualities of plants (especially garlic) are not fully mentioned in scripture when compared with how they were used and practiced in daily life, because such descriptions would detract from belief in God's all-embracing divine power.

Today, garlic continues to be one of the most valuable and useful herbs to have in one's medicine and cosmetic cabinets.

- Garlic is an antibacterial and mucolytic.
- Since ancient times garlic has served as a prophylactic and curative of all sorts of intestinal and respiratory ailments.
- Additionally, garlic is an antiseptic, vermifuge, expectorant, stimulant, stomachic.
- Garlic increases one's resistance to infection.

Garlic in Scripture
Numbers 11.5: The people murmur in the wilderness over food they once ate regularly in Egypt but no longer have access to.

Henna

Lawsonia inermis, better known as henna, has remained constant in its use since ancient times. Henna was primarily a dye with religious, utilitarian, mystical and seductive powers. It was a powerful dark red dye for the hair and a cosmetic dye used to color the tips and nails of fingers and toes. Such colored nails have been observed on some Egyptian mummies. Some believed that henna had a life-giving quality. Because of its pleasant aroma, henna was often wrapped in fine linen and placed in grooves within the body. The fragrance of henna added to its popularity for cosmetic use. It also was included in some Kyphi recipes.

- Today, henna finds use internally and locally for jaundice, leprosy, small pox, and as an emmenagogue.
- Of course henna continues as a dark, reddish brown hair dye and is an excellent hair wash/rinse.
- The leaves of henna, used as a wash, clean up all types of unhealthy skin conditions.
- The essence of henna is prized as perfume oil and in cosmetics.

Henna in Scripture

Song of Solomon 1.14: a cluster of henna blossoms. Emphasizes fragrance.

Song of Solomon 4.13: henna with nard. Another emphasis on beautiful, enticing fragrance.

These references to henna are in an erotic context. Women used henna as a fragrance in their hair and/or their bosoms. Henna hung in bunches from ceilings as a means to purify the air.

Hyssop

Hyssop is a plant that presents a challenge. The hyssop of the Old Testament and of the New Testament are probably not the same plant; moreover, these plants are clearly not the *Hyssopus officinalis* that we know today as hyssop. Some suggest that *Origanum maru* is probably the hyssop of the Old Testament. In fact, this plant seems to work for all scripture references except for John 19.29. Exodus 12.22, which speaks of the preparations for the original Passover, sets the tradition for the balance of references to hyssop: "Take a bunch of hyssop and dip it in the blood which is in the basin, and touch the lintel and the two doorposts with the blood which is in the basin; and none of you shall go out of the door of his house until the morning."

Origanum maru seems most consistent with all of the Biblical references. It is a type of marjoram that people accepted as an herb of protection. The plant was used to cleanse sacred places and in baths of purification. Lepers engaged in a ritual cleansing and used hyssop. The Hebrew word for hyssop is used in the Leviticus and Numbers passages (see below) along with "cedar wood" and "scarlet stuff." In Leviticus, the hyssop combined with cedar wood and scarlet stuff, is dipped in the blood of a sacrificed bird and sprinkled seven times on the person or the house to be cleansed of leprosy. In Numbers, the cedar wood, scarlet stuff and hyssop are burned with the sacrificial red heifer.

Origanum majorana or *Capparis spinosa* have been suggested as other possibilities for the hyssop of Biblical times. The plants grow in the Jordan Valley in Egypt and in the desert in the gorges of Lebanon and Kedron Valley. This "hyssop" works well as an emmenagogue, is excellent for sprains, and also serves as a stimulant, carminative and diaphoretic. It is mildly tonic.

The hyssop of John 19.29 is probably *Sorghum vulgare*, the cane of *dhura*, or Jerusalem corn. This was a central nutritious part of the diet of the people. The reed of this plant was most likely used for the sponge that was lifted up to Jesus. The question is: Did John intentionally use the word hyssop in this setting? Hyssop was a vital part of the redemption theology of the Old Testament. Christ on the cross clearly is a part of the redemption theology of the New Testament. John simply may have been seeking a symbolic meaning or connection between the two redemptive acts.

As mentioned in the opening paragraph of this entry, what is known as hyssop today is not the hyssop of scripture. Today's hyssop is *Hyssopus officinalis*.

- Although completely different, this hyssop is still used by some folks in a redemptive mode, as they use hyssop for purifying those who believe they have sins that need to be forgiven.
- Hyssop has a myriad of medical uses: anticatarrhal, antiasthmatic, anti-inflammatory, antiseptic, emmenagogic, expectorant, sudorific, aromatic, antitussive, astringent and decongestant.

Hyssop in Scripture

Exodus 12.22: marking of the doors in the plague of death that became the Passover observance.

Leviticus 14.4, 6, 49, 51, 52: use of hyssop in the cleansing of leprosy.

Numbers 19.6, 18: purification rites; the rite of the red heifer.

I Kings 4.33: description of Solomon's knowledge. He knows a wide range of things.

Psalm 51.7: Purge me with hyssop. Draws upon the cleansing of leprosy rite in a prayer for healing and moral renewal.

John 19.29: sponge full of vinegar on hyssop for Jesus on the cross. This was probably *Sorghum vulgare*, discussed above.

Hebrews 9.19: sanctifying/cleansing of the people through the sprinkling of blood with a hyssop. This is a reference to Exodus,

Leviticus and Numbers passages, which discuss the sealing of the covenant between God and God's people.

Lotus

Lotus is mentioned only in Job as a plant that provides shade. Lotus was a popular name used for many plants. *Nymphaea lotus* fits the context of Job better than other possibilities; however, *Nymphaea lotus* does not support the linguistic evidence. Using linguistic evidence, *Zizyphus lutea* is preferred.

Lotus has been described as a religious herb used to invoke the gods. Naturally, lotus was found extensively in temples as it was used in religious rituals.

- Jeanne Rose writes that the lotus root (*Nymphaea lotus, Zizyphus lutea*) is used as a cleansing, vaginal douche.
- The flowers are used in perfumery or infused in oil and used for massages as a relaxant.

Lotus in Scripture

Job 40.21, 22: lotus as a shade plant; part of God's second response to Job. God is in control of all forces.

Mallow

According to the Talmud, from 520 B.C. to 516 B.C., the Jews who rebuilt the Temple ate mallows. Winifred Walker, in *All the Plants of the Bible*, describes the mallow as a salt plant eaten as food in cases of dire necessity. The best that can be deduced from various sources is that mallow in the scripture, and from the Biblical times, refers to any plant of the genus, *Malva*. The Interpreter's Dictionary suggests "The association of the Hebrew word with *melah*, 'salt,' along with the LXX equivalent word, and the context of Job 30.4 have led most scholars to identify [mallow] with the *Atriplex halimus*, the 'shrubby orache,' or other similar shrubs common to the salt marshes of the Holy Land." The context of Job 24.24 suggests *Malva sylvestris*, a pink flower that is very prominent in and around Jerusalem during late spring. Some ancients believed mallow helped to develop intellectual skills and moderate passions, and to cleanse the stomach and mind.

Similarity exists in the mallow of Biblical times with that of today, as today's mallow is any plant of the order *Malvaceae*.

- Such plants make soothing emollients that are effective in creams, lotions, decoctions and concoctions, both medicinally and cosmetically.
- Mallow is soothing to mucous membranes and is employed in battling inflammation and irritation of the alimentary canal.
- Mallow also eases the pain of a sore throat as well as the discomfort of indigestion.
- Mallow is a suggested remedy for diarrhea.
- A mallow poultice is good for treating burns and bug bites.

• Mallow serves as a popular remedy for bronchitis and diseases of the chest.

Mallow in Scripture

Job 24.24: Zophar's third discourse; discusses the fate of evil men who wither and fade like mallow. This was most likely *Malva sylvestris*.

Job 30.4: Job's final defense; speaks of mallow as a "last ditch" food. Most likely the *Atriplex halimus*.

Paterson discounts the use of mallow in Job 30.4 but believes it to be the plant referenced in Job 6.6-7 as "white of an egg."

"Can that which is unsavoury be eaten without salt? Or is there any taste in the white of an egg? The things that my soul refused to touch are as my sorrowful meat."
—Job 6.6-7, KJV

"Can that which is tasteless be eaten without salt, or is there any taste in the slime of the purslane? My appetite refuses to touch them; they are as food that is loathsome to me."
—Job 6.6-7, RSV

Melon

Melon is one of the foods mentioned in Numbers 11.5, which the Hebrew people complained of missing as they wandered in the wilderness. What exactly were these melons? Were they *Cucumis melo*, which we recognize as muskmelon? Were they *Citrullus vulgaris*, which we call watermelon? Watermelon has been around "forever" and was once considered the chief food of the poorer people of Egypt. It is cool and refreshing. The same argument can be made for muskmelon.

In *A Modern Herbal: the Medicinal, Culinary, Cosmetic and Economic Properties, Cultivation and Folk-lore of Herbs, Brasses, Fungi, Shrubs & Trees with All Their Modern Scientific Uses*, M. Grieve suggests that the cucumber of Isaiah 1.8 was probably *Cucumis chate* or the "hairy" cucumber, actually a wild melon. Its flesh is similar to that of the common melon and its taste similar to that of the watermelon. Grieve states that *Cucumis chate* was used as a vermicide, an emulsion for catarrh, a purgative, an emetic and for disorder of bowels.

Today's melons are *Cucumis melo, Cucumis cantalupensis, Cucumis dudaim*, and *Cucumis flexuosum*.

- These melons are used with oatmeal and cornmeal, to make cleansing scrubs for skin facials.
- Melon slices are helpful as compresses for sore or tired eyes.

Melon in Scripture

Numbers 11.5: the murmuring scripture. The Israelites bemoan not having food they became accustomed to eating while in slavery in

Egypt.

Isaiah 1.8: The verse speaks of cucumber; however, Grieve, as noted above, suggests that it is the wild melon of Biblical times.

Mint

In the RSV, mint is mentioned only in Matthew and Luke; however, Exodus 12.8 and Numbers 9.11 mention bitter herbs. According to the Talmud, mint is a bitter herb. In addition to being one of the bitter herbs, mint was strewn on the floors of the synagogues to perfume the area with each step a person took.

Ancient cultures believed that mint had health-promoting properties, especially with regard to the digestive and respiratory systems. The ancients used mint as a food, a seasoning, and as a medicine. The most common mint in the Bible lands today is *Mentha longifolia*.

There are about 30 species of mint in the *Lamiaceae* family. For our purposes, we will consider only two: peppermint and spearmint. Peppermint (*Mentha piperita*) has been known and used since the 17th century. It is a viricide, an antibacterial, an expectorant, an anti-spasmodic, a carminative and a stomachic. Spearmint (*Mentha spicata* or *Mentha viridis*) is an anti-emetic, a carminative, an anti-spasmodic, a stimulant and an anti-inflammatory.

- Peppermint serves as a stimulant especially to the heart, brain and pancreas.
- It acts as a powerful painkiller in time of trauma.
- Peppermint eases the discomfort of irritable bowel.
- Peppermint is an anti-inflammatory and an aromatic.
- Tonic, air disinfectant, and mouthwash are other uses for peppermint.
- Spearmint is a tonic for the digestive system and is also good with blends for stress relief.

- Spearmint combats nausea and vomiting.
- As an aromatic, spearmint has a definite place in perfumery and cooking.

Mint in Scripture

Matthew 23.23 and Luke 11.42: Each of these refers to the same setting. Jesus challenges the religious authorities on the laws that they meticulously keep and the human compassion they seem to overlook. This carries an interesting twist, when one considers that mint in its various forms was, and still is, a healing and curative agent. The religious authorities tithed (obeyed the law) mint, a healing plant, but did not extend themselves to offer healing.

Exodus 12.8 and Numbers 9.11: Each of these mentions the bitter herbs that are eaten as part of the Passover meal, and mint is considered among the bitter herbs.

Mustard

Mustard is mentioned only in the sayings of Jesus. Jesus referred to the mustard seed, *Brassica nigra*, to emphasize growth that starts with a very small beginning and expands to a large, world-embracing future. Curiously, some researchers argue that the orchid seed was actually the smallest seed at that time. Jesus' use of mustard seed, mustard tree or shrub seems to allude to Daniel 4.11-12, 30-31, a portion of Nebuchadnezzar's dream. (Verses 11 and 12 speak of a tree that grows mighty in size. Verses 30-31 present Nebuchadnezzar proclaiming his power and glory and God crying out that it is over for Nebuchadnezzar—that which appears to be the mightiest in the land is still subject to God.) In Biblical times, the leaves of the mustard plant were eaten as a vegetable.

The mustard we use today may be either *Brassica alba* or *Brassica nigra*.

- Mustard is an emetic, an irritant and a stimulant.
- *Brassica alba* makes the mustard plasters of common usage to battle chest congestion.
- *Brassica nigra* works wonders in a footbath.
- Oil of mustard is infused ground mustard seed in olive oil and is used as a "snuff" to relieve nasal pain.
- Mustard leaves are good in salads or cooked.

Mustard in Scripture
Matthew 13.31: Jesus teaches in parables "The kingdom of heaven is like a grain of mustard seed."
Matthew 17.20: Jesus heals an epileptic child. "If you have faith as

a grain of mustard seed ..."
Mark 4.31: Jesus teaches in parables. "It is like a grain of mustard seed."
Luke 13.19: parables of mustard seed and leaven. "It is like a grain of mustard seed."
Luke 17.6: forgiveness and faith. "If you had faith as a grain of mustard seed ..."

Myrrh

Most Bible translations use myrrh for Genesis 37.25; 43.11 (*Commiphora myrrha*) but many scholars identify it as the fragrant gum *Cistus creticus*, commonly called rockrose, which is the laudanum of ancient trade. *Commiphora myrrha* is a gum that was sold as a spice or for medicinal purposes. Myrrh was a part of the holy anointing oil. People used it in a salve for the purification of the dead. Myrrh could be found in liquid form as well. In the time of King Solomon, myrrh was used strictly for rituals and especially as part of the sacred incense. Myrrh was part of the cleansing rituals for Hebrew women. In Jesus' time, myrrh was placed in wine given to the condemned as a kind of anesthesia. People employed myrrh as a fumigant, to calm the sick and to make salves.

Cistus creticus was used as a salve, stimulant and expectorant. In fact, some saw this myrrh as a panacea for almost every human affliction from earaches to hemorrhoids. It works internally as an astringent tonic and externally as a cleansing agent.

Clay tablets dating back 4,000 years, with prescriptions written on them calling for myrrh, have been found in the ancient Sumarian town of Nippiu. Myrrh was part of the Kyphi of Egypt.

Ultimately one cannot state with certainty which myrrh was "the myrrh" of scripture. More than 135 species of myrrh grow throughout Africa and Arabia, mostly in arid places. What *is* known is that myrrh played an essential role in the life, well-being and rituals of the people.

- *Commiphora myrrha* is used today as an emmenagogue, an anti-inflammatory that works on the digestive system, an antiviral, an antiseptic and a stomachic.

- Myrrh is an antifungal, especially against candida in the mouth and vagina and in athlete's foot.
- Myrrh is used in cosmetics as well as in some mouthwashes.
- As incense or as part of an incense blend, myrrh brings communion with spiritual awareness.
- Myrrh is an essential ingredient for a heady, rich-smelling incense.

Myrrh in Scripture

Genesis 37.25: caravan of traders. Myrrh is part of ancient trade.

Genesis 43.11: Joseph's brothers return to Egypt, bearing myrrh as part of a gift for the ruler.

Exodus 30.23: Myrrh is part of sacred anointing oil.

I Kings 10.25: part of the gifts that "the whole earth" brought to Solomon as they sought his counsel.

II Chronicles 9.24: similar to the preceding reference.

Esther 2.12: part of the beautification rituals for Hebrew women.

Psalm 45.8: psalm of praise in honor of a young king and his consort. The king's splendor makes an overwhelming impression on the senses.

Proverbs 7.17: Beware of women who try to entice you to bed with myrrh!

Song of Solomon 1.13: Hebrew women were accustomed to wearing little bags of myrrh hanging from their necks between their breasts.

Song of Solomon 3.6: "… like a column of smoke, perfumed with myrrh." Is it a cloud of dust stirred up by the procession, or is it a cloud of smoke from burning incense? Could this be a reference to the "pillar of cloud by day and a pillar of fire by night"? (see Exodus 13.21, 22; 14.19, 24). There is no definitive answer.

Song of Solomon 4.6, 14: "Mountain of myrrh" refers to the girl, a metaphor suggestive of a fertility goddess.

Song of Solomon 5.5, 13: an image of extravagance.

Matthew 2.11: Magi bring myrrh as a gift to the Christ child. This is symbolic of "anointing" as a king and in preparing for death.

Matthew 27.34: RSV and KJV use the word "gall"; however, some ancient writings have myrrh instead of gall.

Mark 15.23: Jesus drank myrrh—the anesthesia for the condemned.
John 19.39: part of Nicodemus' mixture for preparing Jesus' body for entombment.
Revelation 18.13: part of the dirge over the city that is no more, where commerce is no more.

Myrtle

The name "myrtle" is derived from a Greek word meaning perfume and a Hebrew word meaning sweetness. Myrtle was sacred to the goddess Venus. The leafy branches of myrtle—*Myrtis communis*—were used by the Hebrews to cover the booths at the Feast of Succoth. In the writings of Isaiah (the portion scholars refer to as Second Isaiah), myrtle is used as an eschatological symbol. Generally, people viewed myrtle as a symbol for peace as well as a sign of divine blessing or divine generosity. The Greeks crowned priests and heroes with myrtle. Babylonian brides wore garlands of myrtle. The Arabs believed that myrtle was one of three plants taken from the Garden of Eden because of its fragrance.

The fruit of the myrtle is edible and all parts of the plant are fragrant. The people of Bible times used myrtle in oils and perfumes, and as salves.

- Today, *Myrtis communis* finds use as an expectorant and as an antiseptic.
- It is an important soothing agent for eyes.
- Myrtle works well as an aromatic astringent in bath waters.
- It has wide use in perfumery.

Myrtle in Scripture

Nehemiah 8.15: "Make booths as it is written." Leaves are used for booths at the Feast of Succoth.

Isaiah 41.19: part of a "lyrical interlude" between strophes of a writing that speaks of the trial of the nations. Eschatological symbolism. In a time of restoration, nature is transformed.

Isaiah 55.13: a writing extolling the abounding grace of God. Earth is transformed, and nature abounds with a richness of plants and fragrance.

Zechariah 1.8, 10, 11: myrtle trees as location. Scholarship suggests that the Hebrew word was more likely "mountain" instead of myrtle in vv. 8 and 10; and v.11 is probably a gloss.

Nard (Spikenard)

[For use of the words spikenard and nard, see "Choosing the Revised Standard Version of Scripture."]

Nardostachys jatamansi—spikenard, or nard—was imported to the Holy Lands from India. Many believed that nard had mystical powers and therefore served as a fragrance of love. Sometimes nard was mixed with frankincense. Nard was balancing and deeply calming to people. It was used as a strong sedative for the nervous system. Nard was part of the oil for anointing kings and the dead. Extremely expensive, nard was carried in alabaster boxes to preserve the oil. Judas, in John 12.5, remarks, "Why was this ointment not sold for three hundred denarii and given to the poor?" (One denarius equaled one day's wage; one pound of nard was worth three hundred denarri.)

The mention of nard in Song of Solomon reflects the well-documented use of nard and other perfumes in baths and in anointing one's self with perfumed unguents. The use of nard as a love potion made the transfer from India to the Biblical lands. Some scholars suggest that the ointment referred to in Song of Solomon was made from a native aromatic grass, because nard did not reach Palestine until fairly late and Song of Solomon in its present form dates from about the third century B.C. However, the contents of the book actually are much more ancient.

In the Gospel references, we witness a powerful usage of nard. In Mark (and Matthew as well, since Matthew bases his narrative on the Marcan material) the nard is used in contrasting functions of love and death. In an act of deep love and beauty, the unidentified woman poured the nard on the head and hair of Jesus. Given Jesus' pending circumstance, the woman unwittingly anointed "the dead" as well. In John, Mary's act also is one of love, but John uses this narrative to show Jesus being anointed as "king" before entering Jerusalem. After the crucifixion, John presents Nicodemus as anointing Jesus' body with myrrh and aloes. In Luke, nard is assumed to be part of the woman's "professional paraphernalia." The woman of the city who was a sinner was forgiven much by Jesus because of her loving, gracious act of anointing his feet. In a curious twist, in giving the nard, the woman received forgiveness; her emotionally deep sadness was touched and healed.

- We continue to use nard as people in Bible times did: in cosmetic products, as a calming agent, as a powerful oil for grounding, centering and calming.
- Additionally *Nardostachys jatamansi* finds use as an antifungal, expectorant, carminative, anti-infectious and antispasmodic.

Nard in Scripture
Song of Solomon 1.12: fragrance of nard. A product of India, which did not reach Palestine until fairly late. This writing is relatively early. The reference could be to an ointment made from native aromatic grasses.
Song of Solomon 4.13, 14: Nard is part of a listing of beautiful, enticing fragrances that describe a maiden.
Mark 14.3: woman with jar of nard. Anointing, act of love, symbolic of anointing for death.
John 12.3: Mary anointed Jesus with nard. Act of love, symbolic of anointing a king.
Matthew 26.6-13 and Luke 7.36-50: Although these two passages do not mention nard, the use of nard is assumed because of the similarities between them and Mark's account of the event.

Onion

Allium cepa, which is better known to us as the common onion, has been used as a food and seasoning since at least 3000 B.C. Along with garlic, onions were considered a necessary food in the diets of the pyramid builders. Onions have been found in the breasts of mummies and onion peels on the eyes and ears of mummies. Egyptian priests thought the onion symbolized the universe, with the different layers of the onion representing heaven, earth and hell. Ancient medical writings list 26 remedies that mention onion.

This ancient food, seasoning and "medicine" continues in strong use today.

- Onion is a remedy for infections in the lungs or in the gut and is good for improving heart health.
- Onion makes a good poultice for an earache and as a soup is good for a runny nose.
- Onion is used in massage blends for rheumatism.
- It also is an antiseptic, a diuretic and a vulnerary.

Onion/Onions in Scripture

Numbers 11.5: Onions are mentioned in the list of foods that the Israelites murmur about missing as they journey in the wilderness.

Rose

The true rose is not mentioned in scripture except for its use in the Greek name, Rhoda, found in Acts 12.13. In the KJV, Song of Solomon 2.1 speaks of the rose of Sharon. Also in the KJV, Isaiah 35.1 declares, "The wilderness and the solitary place shall be glad for them; and the desert shall rejoice, and blossom as the rose." The RSV uses the same translation as the KJV for Song of Solomon 2.1; however, the RSV notes that the proper word is "crocus" and then uses crocus in Isaiah 35.1.

The true rose was known in ancient Palestine and is mentioned in II Esdras 2.19: "... and the same number of springs flowing with milk and honey, and seven mighty mountains on which roses and lilies grow; by these I will fill your children with joy." This rose was probably *Rose phoenicia*. Other apocryphal references to rose most likely refer to *Nerium oleander*.

Winifred Walker concurs that *Nerium oleander* is the rose of Ecclesiasticus. She does argue that there were other rose species in the area, such as the rose of the water brooks and the rhododendron or rose tree. Walker relates that the *Rose phoenicia* of II Esdras was noted for its sweet perfume and that the *Tulipa sharonensis* is a bulb growing plant.

Rose was used in incense burning for its effect on emotions.

Concerning rose, Jeanne Rose writes, "Of all the scents used in perfumery, that of the Rose is one of the oldest and best known. For thousands of years poets have been inspired by the delightful aroma of this flower. Historians have given many accounts of the methods by which its alluring scent can be captured. One of the earliest references to rose is in the Ayurveda, the series of books on the 'good life' written in ancient Sanskrit that may be 7000 years old. ... There are 5000 varieties of Roses, and of these, only a few are called 'Old Roses' and are used for the extraction of scent."

- The flower, rose, encourages contentment and inner vision.
- It soothes emotional shock; it is uplifting.
- Rose is found in many cosmetics and body care products.
- Rose also is an astringent, antidepressant, antiseptic and a nerve tonic.
- It works on asthma, and can be stimulating.

Rose in Apocryphal Literature

Ecclesiasticus 24.14: "... like rose plants in Jericho."

Ecclesiasticus 39.13: "... and bud like a rose growing by a stream of water."

Ecclesiaticus 50.8: "... like roses in the days of the first fruits."

Enoch 106.2, 10: "And his body was white as snow and red as the blooming of a rose, and the hair of his head and his long locks were white as wool and his eyes beautiful. ... And now, my father, hear me: unto Lamech my son there hath been born a son, the like of whom there is none, and his nature is not like man's nature, and the colour of his body is whiter than snow and redder than the bloom of a rose, and the hair of his head is whiter than white wool, and his eyes are like the rays of the sun, and he opened his eyes and thereupon lighted up the whole house."

II Esdras 2.19: "... seven mighty mountains on which roses and lilies grow."

Rose in Scripture

As noted in the text above, *rose* does appear in the RSV in **Song of Solomon 2.1**. However, a text footnote indicates that the preferable translation is "crocus." Also noted above are the verses in the apocryphal writings that refer to rose and which, in fact, translate as "rose."

Rue

Rue is found only in Luke—in Jesus' challenge of the religious authorities' practices on tithing of herbs but neglect of human compassion. Scholars argue that dill was probably the original and correct word, rather than rue. However, rue was a plant of Biblical lands. Rue (*Ruta graveolens*) as a disinfectant was scattered in the courts of justice to protect the officers from prison fever as well as to cover the stench created by prisoners.

Pliny describes rue as a valuable herb and recounts 84 remedies containing rue. Rue was used as a preventative against contagious diseases and for insect and snakebites. Women ate rue leaves as a contraceptive.

Rue once grew quite commonly around the temples at Rome, and people believed it to be an herb of protection for home and family. The Federal Drug Administration considers rue oil to be safe to humans as it is currently used in food flavorings. One must always use rue with caution: *It should never be used nor taken to excess, for there is a potential of rue poisoning.* Rue should be *avoided* during pregnancy.

- Rue is used as an emmenagogue, a stimulant, an antispasmodic and a rubefacient.
- In wine growing areas, rue leaves are put in brandy to produce liqueur, which is used to aid digestion.
- Some use rue as a disinfectant.
- Rue also has been successful in warding off attacks of fleas and various insects.

Rue in Scripture
Luke 11.42: " … you tithe mint, rue …"

Saffron

In Biblical times, saffron (*Crocus sativus*) was strewn in public theaters and fountains to generate a sweet scent. It was used as a gastric and intestinal remedy, and also as an antiflatulent. Saffron was integral to cooking as a condiment, both for its flavoring qualities and coloring properties. Saffron also was used as a perfume and a dye.

For the Persians, saffron is seen as a very strong magical substance that accompanies religious rites.

- Today, *Crocus sativus* is used as a carminative, diaphoretic and an emmenagogue.
- Saffron serves as the water-soluble red dye in some cosmetics and hair rinses, salves and lotions.

Saffron in Scripture

Song of Solomon 4.14: Listed with the sweet perfumes used to describe the young maiden.

Terebinth

The terebinth of the Bible and terebinth of today are probably not the same thing. In the scripture, terebinth was either *Pistacia terebinthus* or *Pistacia palastina*. It was called the "turpentine tree" or "teil tree." The wood apparently was hard and white. It was a good shade tree. Perhaps the tree of Judges 6.11, which speaks of an oak tree, was the terebinth.

Terebinth is not often used therapeutically in the United States. The French use it as:

- an antiseptic, expectorant, as a stimulant, and to oxygenate blood after an ozone treatment.
- Pine oil and turpentine make a powerful germicide for respiratory catarrh and infections.
- It is good to inhale for fainting spells.
- Terebinth can scent a room and clean the air.
- Terebinth is good for vaginal problems.
- Taken internally terebinth is effective against all sorts of hemorrhage and can kill tapeworm.

Terebinth in Scripture

Isaiah 6.13: from the call of Isaiah to be a prophet.
Hosea 4.13: Shade is good. Make offering under shade trees.

Wormwood

The KJV uses wormwood more than does the RSV. The LXX never used wormwood, choosing instead to use the word "bitterness." Wormwood became a metaphor for bitterness or sorrow. Wormwood has a very bitter taste so some have assumed that wormwood is the gall that is mentioned in scripture. All in all, no one really knows for certain what the Biblical wormwood really was. Apparently, whatever wormwood was, it was steeped into wine to counteract the effects of alcohol. It has been in use since about 600 B.C. as a religious herb among the Greeks and Hebrews. Wormwood was used to banish anger and negative energy. The "best guess" is that wormwood is *Artemisia spp.*, or perhaps *Artemisia herba-alba.*

- Today's wormwood is Artemisia absinthium and is used to manufacture absinthe.
- Wormwood contains thujone, which is toxic; therefore, it should not be used in therapy either externally or internally.

Since many scholars assume that wormwood is the "gall" mentioned in scripture, herewith is a list of the occurrences of gall in the RSV:

Job 16.13: "... he pours out my gall on the ground."

Job 20.14, 25: "... it is the gall of the asps within him. ... the glittering point comes out of his gall. ..."

Lamentations 3.19: "Remember my affliction and my bitterness, the wormwood and the gall!"

Matthew 27.34: "They offered him wine to drink, mingled with gall. ..."

Acts 8.23: "For I see that you are in the gall of bitterness and in the bond of iniquity."

Wormwood in Scripture

Proverbs 5.4: "She is bitter as wormwood."
Jeremiah 9.15: "Feed people wormwood." This passage discusses the destruction of Jerusalem. God is disturbed with Israel and will give them bitter medicine.
Jeremiah 23.15: "Feed them with wormwood." The prophets of Jerusalem have sinned mightily, and once again God will give bitter medicine to the people.
Lamentation 3.15, 19: A personal lament, lifting some bitter experiences from life.
Amos 5.7: "Turn justice to wormwood." Amos decries the brutal miscarriage of justice by the privileged over the less fortunate.
Amos 6.12: Once again, Amos decries the corruption of justice.
Revelation 8.11: This perhaps refers to Jeremiah 9.15 and Jeremiah 23.15, where God gave bitter medicine to the people, a "medicine" that may be prescribed again.

Part III:
Appendices

Appendix 1

Herbs & Plants Mentioned In the Papyrus Ebers

The Papyrus Ebers was written around 1500 B.C., with some of the "recipes" within it dating from about 3500 B.C. These prescriptions established an early standard for treatment. Following is a list of plants mentioned in the prescriptions of the Papyrus Ebers that are also discussed in this text.

- Aloes, grain of aloes, resin of aloes, wood of aloes
- Balsam, real balsam
- Cassia
- Cedar tree, fat of the cedar tree, splinters of the cedar tree, tops of the cedar tree
- Coriander, coriander berries
- Cucumber, flowers of the cucumber
- Cyprus [sic] from the North, from the fields, from the meadow, from the marshes, knots of cyprus, thorns of the cyprus, cyprus grass
- Figs
- Garlic
- Bread of the Zizyphus lotus
- Resin of the Zizyphus lotus
- Splinters of the Zizyphus lotus
- Wood of the Zizyphus lotus
- Mint of the mountains
- Myrrh, dried myrrh, sweet myrrh, oil of myrrh

- Olive oil
- Onions, fresh onions, green onions, onions from the oasis, onion meal, inner of onion, sap of fresh onion
- Blossoms of peppermint
- Saffron, saffron seeds, blossoms of the saffron
- Watermelon
- Wormwood

Appendix 2

Ailments & Pathologies Addressed in the Papyrus Ebers

The 811 prescriptions in the Papyrus Ebers address over 80 illnesses, conditions and pathologies. Many of these are recognizable as common illnesses today; others have a curious ring to them. The following is a sampling of those pathologies.

- Headache
- Migraine
- Giddiness
- Constipation
- Diarrhea
- Indigestion
- Colic
- Dysentery
- Tapeworms
- Roundworms
- Enlarged Prostate
- Stone
- Cardiac pain and weakness
- Diseases of the liver
- Baldness
- Alopecia
- Eczema

- Impetigo
- Stings of Wasps and Tarantulae
- Bite of a Crocodile
- Burns of the First, Second, Third, Fourth and Fifth Day
- Menstrual irregularities
- Diseases of the Breasts
- Falling of the Womb
- Deafness
- Cancer
- Inflammations

Appendix 3

Scripture References by Word

Additional Essential Oils and Related Words
Traced Through the Revised Standard Version of the Bible

Anoint (anointed, anointest, anointing)   Aroma
Evergreen   Fir
Fragrance (fragrant)   Incense
Odor/s   Oil/s
Olive oil   Onycha
Pine   Spice/s
Stacte

In addition to the 35 words considered in the body of this paper, another 13 words are included here and in the following appendix. These words are offered as an aid to those interested in doing additional scripture research on words associated with essential oils, naturopathy or aromatherapy. If one were to compare the information shared here with similar listings in a concordance of the Revised Standard Version of the Bible, one would find some discrepancies, i.e., some scriptural references found in a concordance are not included in this appendix under some words. Those scripture references that are not included were determined as not relevant to the theme of this book. As an example, *Nelson's Complete Concordance of the Revised Standard Version* contains 28 references for the word *anointing*. This work lists 16. These 16 references refer to *anointing oil*, which is usually a sacred or holy oil, clearly a relevant topic of concern. The other 12 uses of *anointing* refer to the physical act of anointing someone or as descriptive of a type of teaching.

Anoint

Exodus 29.7: anoint with oil; Aaron
Exodus 30.30: anoint Aaron
Exodus 40.9, 10, 11, 13, 15: anoint altar, utensils, Aaron
Ruth 3.3: Ruth to anoint self to meet Boaz
I Samuel 9.16: anoint individual
I Samuel 15.1: Samuel to anoint Saul
I Samuel 16.3: anoint for me one who I name
I Samuel 16.12: arise, anoint [David]
I Kings 1.34: anoint him king over Israel
I Kings 19.15, 16: anoint various people as kings
II Kings 9.3, 6: flask of oil … anoint king over Israel
Amos 6.6: woe…anoint selves with finest oils
Micah 6.15: not anoint with oil
Matthew 6.17: when fast, anoint head, wash face
Mark 16.1: Mary, Mary Magdalene, Salome…anoint body
Luke 7.46: did not anoint head, anointed feet
Acts 4.27: Jesus whom thou didst anoint
Revelation 3.18: anoint eyes that you may see

Anointed

Numbers 35.25: high priest anointed with holy oil
I Samuel 16.13: Samuel took horn of oil and anointed him
I Kings 1.39: priest took horn of oil and anointed Solomon
Psalm 45.7: God has anointed you with oil of gladness
Psalm 89.20: with my holy oil I have anointed him
Isaiah 61.1: Spirit of Lord upon me because God has anointed me
Ezekiel 16.9: bathed you with water and washed off your blood from you and anointed you with oil
Mark 6.13: and anointed with oil many that were sick and healed them
Mark 14.8: she has anointed my body

Luke 4.18: Jesus reading scripture and refers to Isaiah 61.1 "God has anointed me"
Luke 7.38, 46: woman of the city, alabaster…anointed feet
John 9.6, 11: anointed man's eye with the clay
John 11.2: Jesus refers to John 12.3
John 12.3: Mary anointed Jesus' feet

There are 95 occurrences of *anointed* in the RSV, sixteen are cited here. The balance of the references speak of "anointed one" or else *anointed* is used as a verb without the mention of oil. What seems to stand out in the above references is the sense of healing (see especially Ezekiel 16.9, Mark 6.13, John 9.6, 11), whether that healing is a physical healing or healing in spirit or soul.

Anointest
Psalm 23.5: thou anointest my head with oil – a sense of healing, comfort, wholeness

Anointing
Exodus 25.6: spices for anointing oil
Exodus 29.7: took the anointing oil
Exodus 29.21: of the anointing oil and sprinkle it
Exodus 30.25: a sacred anointing oil blended…holy anointing oil it shall be
Exodus 31.11: the anointing oil and the fragrant
Exodus 35.8, 15, 28: spices for anointing oil…anointing oil and fragrant…for the anointing oil
Exodus 37.29: he made the holy anointing oil
Exodus 39.38: the anointing oil and the fragrant incense
Exodus 40.9, 15: anointing oil to anoint tabernacle…serve as priests
Leviticus 8.2, 10, 12, 30: ordination of priests anointing oil used
Leviticus 10.7: anointing oil of the Lord upon you
Leviticus 21.10, 12: chief priest upon whose head the anointing oil is poured
Numbers 4.16: have oversight of the anointing oil

Song of Solomon 1.3: your anointing oils are fragrant
James 5.14: pray…anointing him with oil

Aroma

II Corinthians 2.15: aroma of Christ to God. Reminiscent of the fragrances of the incense and the burnt offerings offered to God; as God could detect the aroma of those offerings, so God detects the aroma of these people who follow and serve Jesus "the aroma of Christ to God"

Evergreen
Hosea 14.8: evergreen cypress

Fir
Psalm 104.17: stork has home in fir tree—in praise of the Creator
Ezekiel 27.5: fir with cedar—lament over Tyre; good ship built with cedar and fir
Ezekiel 31.8: fir with cedars—part of the allegory of the cedar

Evergreen and fir are included here because each of the references connects with another referenced plant (cypress, cedar). Also some aromatherapy books do extensive discussions on fir and/or evergreen trees. These verses indicate that there is little within the scripture (at least in the RSV) to merit more in-depth consideration.

Fragrance
Song of Solomon 1.12: nard…fragrance
Song of Solomon 2.13: figs…fragrance
Song of Solomon 4.10: fragrance oil better than spice
Song of Solomon 4.16: wind, garden, fragrance
Song of Solomon 5.13:…like beds of spices yielding fragrance
Song of Solomon 7.13: mandrakes…fragrance
Hosea 14.6, 7: reborn Israel fragrance like Lebanon
John 12.3: Mary, nard, anointed Jesus' feet…fragrance

II Corinthians 2.14, 16: fragrance of the knowledge of Christ, fragrance death to death, life to life

Pleasing odors are clearly the primary theme in the use of fragrance. An interesting twist is found in the Hosea passage. Several prophets, among them being Amos, spoke of God's displeasure with the fragrance of the Israelites' offerings because the people were meticulous in keeping ritual, but abysmal in caring for the widow and the orphan, the least, the lost, and the lonely, as the law required them to do. In Hosea, Israel seems to have gotten "back on track," and the fragrance of the people is once again pleasing to God. The II Corinthians passage continues the thought discussed under *aroma*. The ways of the people who follow the teachings of Jesus are a pleasing fragrance to God and to those around them who witness their lives.

Fragrant
Exodus 25.6: fragrant incense
Exodus 30.7: fragrant incense
Exodus 31.11: fragrant oil and incense
Exodus 35.8: anointing oil and fragrant incense
Exodus 35.15: anointing oil and fragrant incense
Exodus 35.28: anointing oil and fragrant incense
Exodus 37.29: fragrant incense
Exodus 39.38: anointing oil and fragrant incense
Exodus 40.27: fragrant incense
Leviticus 4.7: fragrant incense
Numbers 4.16: fragrant incense
Psalm 45.8: robes fragrant with myrrh
Song of Solomon 1.3: anointing oil fragrant
Song of Solomon 3.6: fragrant powders (Hepper suggests that this might be *opobalsumum*)
Ephesians 5.2: Christ gave self up as fragrant offering
Philippians 4.18: fragrant offering

The Exodus, Leviticus and Numbers passages speak of worship rituals and settings; the fragrant incense provides a fragrant odor to God. The epistle passages (Ephesians and Philippians) draw upon the imagery of the Old Testament/Pentateuch of being a pleasing odor/fragrant offering to God. Jesus was the offering, not a sacrificed sheep or bird or bull, or even some holy incense; the offering was Christ himself.

Incense

Exodus 25.6: give as an offering
Exodus 25.29: making plates for incense
Exodus 30.1, 7, 8, 9, 27: altar; offer perpetual offering
Exodus 30.35, 37: a blended incense
Exodus 31.8, 11: altar of incense; fragrant incense
Exodus 35.8, 15, 28: offering...fragrant incense, altar of incense
Exodus 37.16, 25, 29: dishes for incense; altar of incense of acacia wood, blended
Exodus 39.38: anointing oil and fragrant incense
Exodus 40.5, 27: golden altar for incense; burnt fragrant incense as Lord commanded
Leviticus 4.7: blood on the horns of the altar of fragrant incense
Leviticus 10.1: laid incense on censer, unholy for . . .
Leviticus 16.12, 13: offering as part of Day of Atonement
Levitius 26.30: cut down incense altars
Numbers 4.7: incense dish on table of bread of presence
Numbers 4.16: process leading up to fragrant incense
Numbers 7.14, 20, 26, 32, 38, 44, 50, 56, 62, 68, 74, 80, 86: part of offering from each tribal leader
Numbers 16.7, 17, 18, 35, 40, 46, 47: men offering incense to God, God consumes them with fire; warning
Deuteronomy 33.10: part of blessing of Moses, Levites to be priests, burning incense
I Samuel 2.28: call of Samuel and one task is to burn incense
I Kings 3.3: Solomon burned incense
I Kings 7.50: dishes for incense in temple

I Kings 9.25: Solomon three times a year burning incense
I Kings 11.8: Solomon burned incense for his foreign wives
I Kings 12.33: Jereboam's idolatry
I Kings 13.1, 2: continuation of Jereboam's idolatry
I Kings 22.43: the people still sacrificed and burned incense on the high places
II Kings 12.3: still people burned incense in high places committing idolatry
II Kings 14.4: still people burned incense in high places committing idolatry
II Kings 15.4, 35: still people burned incense in high places committing idolatry
II Kings 16.4: Ahaz king of Israel burned incense in wrong place
II Kings 17.11: burning incense in high places committing idolatry
II Kings 18.4: Hezekiah's reform
II Kings 22.17: idolatry
II Kings 23.5, 8: punishing priest who burned incense to idols
II Kings 25.14: fall of Jerusalem, temple ransacked, dishes for incense taken away
I Chronicles 6.49: lineage of Levites, Aaron offers offering on altar of incense for atonement
I Chronicles 9.29: genealogy of families returning and one family has oversight of oil, incense, spices
I Chronicles 23.13: Levites organize and this tribe has responsibility for incense
I Chronicles 28.18: instruction for how temple altar of incense to be built
II Chronicles 2.4, 6: Solomon to build temple, place burning incense to God
II Chronicles 4.22: dishes for incense
II Chronicles 13.11: Abijah properly offers incense of spices
II Chronicles 14.5: destruction of altar of incense for idolatry
II Chronicles 24.14: Joash restoration of temple and altar of incense
II Chronicles 26.16, 18, 19: Uzziah burned incense to God instead of priests doing it so is punished

II Chronicles 28.3, 4, 25: Ahaz burns incense to idols
II Chronicles 29.7, 11: improper use; proper use of temple burning incense
II Chronicles 30.14: altar of incense
II Chronicles 34.4, 7, 25: break down altar of incense to Baal, people burnt incense to idols
Psalm 141.2: let prayer be counted as incense
Isaiah 1.13: oracle incense is abomination
Isaiah 17.8: oracle against tribes
Isaiah 27.9: no…incense altars will remain standing
Isaiah 65.3, 7: nature cult practice
Jeremiah 1.16: incense burned to idols
Jeremiah 11.12, 13, 17: burning incense to Baal
Jeremiah 18.15: false gods burn incense
Jeremiah 19.4, 13: burning incense to false gods
Jeremiah 32.29: incense burned to Baal
Jeremiah 41.5: burning incense
Jeremiah 44.3, 5, 8, 15, 17, 18, 19, 21, 23, 25: burning incense to idols and to the "queen of heaven"
Jeremiah 48.35: burning incense to idols
Jeremiah 52.18, 19: Jerusalem burned and despoiled and dishes for incense taken
Ezekiel 6.4, 6: altar of incense cut down because of idolatry
Ezekiel 8.11: elders burning incense committing idolatry
Ezekiel 16.18: Jerusalem's unfaithfulness
Ezekiel 23.41: Israel's apostasy idolatrous incense burning
Daniel 2.46: Nebuchadnezzar; incense offering to Daniel and Daniel's God
Hosea 2.13: burning incense to Baal
Hosea 11.2: burning incense to idols
Habakkuk 1.16: profane worship
Malachi 1.11: offering incense to God
Luke 1.9, 10, 11: Zechariah burning incense properly
Hebrews 9.4: refers to golden altar of incense of Hebrew people
Revelation 5.8: prayers joined with incense

Revelation 8.3, 4: prayers, incense, smoke
Revelation 18.13: fallen city, commerce no more, incense not traded

Gums and resins were used in incense, especially in the holy incense. A number of plants were used in some way as aromatics or in incense. Clearly, from all of these scripture references we can see how critical incense and fragrance were to the faith lives of the Biblical people. Also very clear is the people's propensity for misusing the incense—burning it improperly, in improper places, to inappropriate gods. If we have any familiarity with the prophets, especially the eighth century prophets—Isaiah, Amos, and Hosea— we know how often and how strongly they decried the empty rituals of the people, which included the burning of fragrant offerings and incense. The people were good in ritual and empty on justice issues. Perhaps it is in part the reason that incense-burning has waned in religious traditions, particularly within denominations grounded in the reformation tradition and in churches that emerged out of the great awakening and revival periods. Yet incense burned properly and/or offered properly enhanced the religious experience of the people. Incense continues to do so in the Roman and Orthodox traditions.

Incense can play a significant role in the work of the aromatherapist and/or naturopath. The fragrance from the burning incense aids in healing and in spiritual journeys.

Odor/s

Genesis 8.21: Noah's burnt offering…a pleasing odor
Exodus 29.18: whole ram burnt offering…a pleasing odor
Exodus 29.25: burnt offering…a pleasing odor
Exodus 29.41: lamb, cereal offering…a pleasing odor
Leviticus 1.9, 13, 17: three different burnt offerings…a pleasing odor
Leviticus 2.2, 9: cereal and burn it…pleasing odor
Leviticus 2.12: fruit not to be burned…not to be offered on the altar as a pleasing odor

Leviticus 3.5, 16: peace offerings...a pleasing odor to the Lord
Leviticus 4.31: fat from peace offering...a pleasing odor to the Lord
Leviticus 6.15: cereal and frankincense...a pleasing odor to the Lord
Leviticus 6.21: cereal offering...pleasing odor to the Lord
Leviticus 8.21: ram burnt offering...a pleasing odor to the Lord
Leviticus 8.28: wave offering, burnt offering, ordination offering...a pleasing odor to the Lord
Leviticus 17.6: peace offering...a pleasing odor to the Lord
Leviticus 23.13: lamb and cereal offerings...a pleasing odor to the Lord
Leviticus 23.18: seven lambs, one bull, two rams and cereal and drink offering...pleasing odor
Leviticus 26.31: lay waste and not smell pleasing odors
Numbers 15.3, 7, 10, 13, 14, 24: burnt, drink, lamb offerings... pleasing odor
Numbers 18.17: firstling, fat offering...pleasing odor
Numbers 28.2: burnt offering...pleasing odor
Numbers 28.6: Sinai, continual burnt offering...pleasing odor
Numbers 28.8: offering by fire...pleasing odor
Numbers 28.13: flour and oil like cereal offering...pleasing odor
Numbers 28.24: the food of an offering by fire ... pleasing odor
Numbers 28.27: burnt offering...pleasing odor
Numbers 29.2: burnt offering...pleasing odor
Numbers 29.6: a variety of offerings described...pleasing odor
Numbers 29.8: burnt offering...pleasing odor
Numbers 29.13: details of a burnt offering...pleasing odor
Numbers 29. 36: details of a burnt offering...pleasing odor
Ecclesiastes 10.1: perfumer's ointment give off an evil odor
Ezekiel 6.13: wherever they offered pleasing odor to all their idols
Ezekiel 16.19: bread, flour, oil and honey...pleasing odor
Ezekiel 20.28: sacrificed to idols and sent up their soothing odor (not good in this case)
Ezekiel 20.41: as a pleasing odor I will accept you

Providing pleasing odors through proper offerings was an integral part of the religious life of the Israelites. Sending up a pleasing odor through offerings made to idols and false gods was not a proper use of pleasing odors, and God would send punishment. Odor, aroma and fragrance played a significant part in the daily life of the Israelites.

Oil/s

Genesis 28.18: Jacob, stone, dream, consecrate with oil
Genesis 35.14: pillar which Jacob consecrates with oil
Exodus 25.6: lamp oil and anointing oil
Exodus 27.20: olive oil for light
Exodus 29.7, 21, 40: anointing oil, beaten oil part of offering
Exodus 30.24, 25, 31: creating a sacred anointing oil
Exodus 31.11: anointing oil
Exodus 35.8, 15, 28: anointing oil
Exodus 37.29: anointing oil
Exodus 39.38: anointing oil
Exodus 40.9: anointing oil to consecrate temple furniture
Leviticus 2.1, 2, 5-7, 15, 16: part of cereal offering with flour and frankincense
Leviticus 5.11: sin offering has no oil, no frankincense
Leviticus 6.15, 21: cereal offering with flour, oil, frankincense
Leviticus 7.10, 12: cereal offering, thank offering with oil
Leviticus 8.2, 10, 12, 30: anointing oil
Leviticus 8.26: bread with oil
Leviticus 9.4: cereal offering with oil
Leviticus 10.7: anointing oil
Leviticus 14.10, 12, 15-18, 21, 24, 26-29: cleansing of lepers, cereal offering with oil, log of oil, putting oil on hand, ear for cleansing
Leviticus 21.10, 12: anointing oil makes priests holy to God
Leviticus 23.13: part of cereal offering
Numbers 4.16: anointing oil
Numbers 5.15: cereal offering of jealousy, no oil
Numbers 6.15: sacrifice, flour oil, wafers with oil
Numbers 7.13, 19, 25, 31, 37, 43, 49, 55, 61, 73, 79: cereal offering each tribal leader gave with oil

Numbers 8.8: cereal offering with oil
Numbers 15.4, 6, 9: cereal offering with oil
Numbers 18.12: best of oil given as gift
Numbers 28.5, 9, 12, 13, 20, 28: cereal offering
Numbers 29.3, 9, 14: cereal offering
Deuteronomy 12.17: do not eat the tithe of oil
Deuteronomy 14.23: can eat tithe of oil
Deuteronomy 18.4: first fruits oil
Deuteronomy 33.24: blessing Ashar
I Samuel 10.1: vial of oil to anoint
I Samuel 16.13: horn of oil to anoint
II Samuel 14.2: do not anoint self with oil
I Kings 1.39: horn of oil to anoint
II Kings 9.1, 3, 6: pouring oil to anoint Jehu
II Kings 20.13: precious oil
I Chronicles 9.29: returning exiles appointed charge over oil
I Chronicles 23.29: offering mixed with oil
II Chronicles 31.5: first fruits oil
Ezra 6.9: oil as priests require
Nehemiah 10.37, 39: contribution of oil
Nehemiah 13.5: tithe of oil '
Esther 2.12: oil of myrrh
Psalm 23.5: anoint head with oil
Psalm 45.7: anoint with oil of gladness
Psalm 89.20: with my oil have anointed David
Psalm 104.15: oil to make face shine, part of God's blessings upon children of God
Psalm 133.2: precious oil
Proverbs 27.9: oil and perfume make heart glad
Song of Solomon 1.3: anointing oils…your name is oil poured out
Song of Solomon 4.10: the fragrance of your oils
Isaiah 39.2: precious oil
Isaiah 57.9: you journeyed to Molech with oil
Isaiah 61.3: oil of gladness
Ezekiel 16.9: anointed with oil

Ezekiel 16.18, 19: oil and incense, food, pleasing odor
Ezekiel 23.41: incense and oil
Ezekiel 45.14, 24, 25: parts of offerings
Ezekiel 46.5, 7, 11, 14, 15: parts of offerings
Amos 6.6: anointing with oil
Micah 6.7: rivers of oil
Micah 6.15: not anoint selves with oil
Mark 6.13: disciples anoint others with oil
Luke 7.46: did not anoint head with oil but she
Luke 10.34: good Samaritan bound up wounds with oil and wine
Hebrews 1.9: anointed with oil of gladness
James 5.14: anointing sick with oil
Revelation 18.13: destruction, end of commerce

Olive oil
Exodus 27.20: pure beaten olive oil for the light
Exodus 30.24: and of olive oil a hin

Olive oil and almond oil were the preferred oils of the people in Biblical times.

Onycha
Exodus 30.34: onycha as part of the blended incense

Pine
Song of Solomon 1.17: rafters are pine
Isaiah 41.19: put in wilderness
Isaiah 60.13: beautify place

Aromatherapy books often discuss pine and pine oils. Pine mentioned in scripture refers strictly to wood.

Spice/s
Exodus 25.6: spices for the anointing oil
Exodus 30.23: finest spices for a sacred anointing oil

Exodus 30.34: sweet spices to make blended incense pure and holy (Hepper suggests that this might be *balsum*)
Exodus 35.8: spices for the anointing oil
Exodus 35.28: spices and oil for the light and for the anointing oil
I Kings 10.2, 10, 25: Queen of Sheba's visit and gifts she brings including spices
II Kings 20.13: Hezekiah welcomed them with gifts…spices
I Chronicles 9.29, 30: those who had charge over spices and responsible for mixing spices
II Chronicles 2.4: burning of incense of sweet spices
II Chronicles 9.1, 9, 24: Queen of Sheba's visit, bringing spices
II Chronicles 13.11: offer…burnt offerings and incense of sweet spices
II Chronicles 16.14: kind of spices prepared by perfumer's art
II Chronicles 32.27: Hezekiah made for himself treasure of…sweet spices
Esther 2.12: six months with oil, six months with spices in period of beautification
Song of Solomon 4.10:…fragrance of your oils better than any spice
Song of Solomon 4.14: list of chief spices used to describe young maiden
Song of Solomon 5.1:…I gather my myrrh with my spice …
Song of Solomon 5.13: cheeks like bed of sweet spices—maiden searches for her lover
Song of Solomon 6.2:…the bed of spices …
Song of Solomon 8.14:…be like a…young stag up on the mountains of spices
Isaiah 39.2: Hezekiah treasures of spices
Jeremiah 34.5: spices burned for ancestors…so burn spices for you
Ezekiel 27.22: traders of Sheba and Ramah trade all kinds of spices
Mark 16.1: women brought spices to anoint body of Jesus
Luke 23.56: women prepared spices for body of Jesus
Luke 24.1: spices the women had prepared
John 19.40: took body of Jesus and bound it in spices
Revelation 18.13: cinnamon, spice, incense, trading no longer

possible

Stacte

Exodus 30.34: stacte, onycha, galbanum, part of a blended incense

Appendix 4

Scripture References by Book of the Bible

Essential Oils and Related Words
Traced Through the Revised Standard Version of the Bible

This appendix will be of particular interest to those individuals who seek more of a Biblical perspective on the references, and how that perspective may connect with an aromatherapy perspective. It traces the same words as listed in the previous appendix, plus the essential oils discussed in Section II. Here, however, the references are listed according to the books of the Bible. What words appear in Genesis? What words appear in Luke? Are there any books of the Bible that do not contain any of the words researched for this book? Those answers and information are to be found in this section.

Almond/s	Aloes	Anoint (anointed, anointest, anointing)	
Apple	Aroma	Balm	Balsam
Bdellium	Calamus	Cassia	Cedar/s
Cedarwood	Cinnamon	Coriander	Cucumber
Cumin/Cummin	Cypress/es	Dill	Evergreen
Fir	Fig	Fragrance (fragrant)	
Frankincense	Galbanum	Garlic	Henna
Hyssop	Incense	Lotus	Mallow
Melon	Mint	Mustard	Myrrh
Myrtle	Nard (Spikenard)		Odor/s
Oil/s	Olive oil	Onions	Onycha
Pine	Rose	Rue	Saffron
Spice/s	Stacte	Terebinth	Wormwood

GENESIS

2.12 bdellium: description of land bdellium and onyx stone are there—part of the description of the "geography" of the world, a separation of the earthly waters (a parallel to Genesis 1 and the separation of the waters in creation). Here the emphasis is upon horizontal separation compared to the vertical separation in creation, how the earth's geography is formed and sections are noted by its stones, plants, etc.[1]

3.7 fig: Adam and Eve sew fig leaves together—even though their eyes are opened, nothing really new to see but now see their true status. What they see is not their expected autonomy; what is seen is their guilt and the fact that they are naked and that is a disappointment.[2, 3]

8.21 odor: Noah's burnt offering. In Genesis 6.5-7 God saw evil in human heart and resolved to destroy humanity; in 8.21 God still sees evil in humankind's heart but chooses to preserve humankind; God's attitude has changed toward creation and toward what is appropriate judgment[4]; God smelled the odor, a daring anthropomorphism, which was a significant part of the ancient tradition of Israel.[5]

28.18 oil: Jacob, stone, dream, consecrate

30.37 almond: fresh rods of poplar and almond and …

35.14 oil: pillar, which Jacob consecrates

37.25 balm, myrrh: caravan with Joseph—balm and myrrh are used both for healing and at death in embalming, the narrative provides a progression of three courses of action: immediate death, 37.20; delayed death, 37.21-22; slavery, 37.27-28.[6]

43.11 balm, myrrh, almonds: Joseph's brothers return to Egypt with balm…myrrh…almonds. The irony is that by sending gifts, Jacob once again unwittingly shows preferential treatment to Joseph; also irony that the gifts sent are among the very things Ishmaelites had when they bought Joseph years earlier.[7]

EXODUS

12.8 bitter herbs: The implication is that this includes mint. Later Jewish tradition specified that there were five herbs and these herbs were "spiritualized" to reflect the Egyptian bondage.[8]

12.22 hyssop: marking for Passover

16.31 coriander: description of manna. Another suggestion is that the shape of manna is like that of a coriander seed but is white in color.[9]

25.6 incense, fragrant, spices, anointing oil: give as an offering, lamp oil and spices for anointing oil

25.29 incense: making plates and dishes for

25.32-36 almonds: cups made like almonds with capitals and flowers. The almond tree is the first to blossom in the spring; the white petals represent new life that follows after the cold, dormant winter; Israel experiences it as symbolizing "God's wakefulness"; the lamp stands also are seen as "tree of life" of Genesis; in these stands, with the almond carving Israel sees light, life and presence.[10]

These verses in chapter 25 give exact directions for the incense and for making offerings and other aspects that pertain to offerings in the tabernacle.[11]

27.20 oil, olive oil: olive oil for light

29.7 anoint, anointing, anoint with oil: anointing Aaron

29.18 odor: whole ram burnt offering

29.21 anointing, of the anointing oil

29.25 odor: burnt offering

29.41 odor: lamb, cereal offering

29.7, 21, 40 oil, anointing, anointing oil, hin of beaten oil

30.1,7,8, 9, 27 incense, fragrant: altar, offer perpetual offering

30.23 cinnamon, myrrh, spices: sacred anointing oil, finest spices

30.24, 25, 31 cassia, oil, anointing, olive oil: part of priestly matters, used in making sacred oil

30.30 anoint: anoint Aaron

30.34 frankincense, galbanum, spices, stacte, onycha: make an incense pure and holy; sweet spices stacte and onycha

30.35, 37 incense: a blended incense

31.8, 11 incense, fragrant, anointing oil: altar of incense, fragrant incense, anointing oil

35.8, 15, 28 incense, oil, fragrant, anointing: offering…fragrant incense, altar of incense and fragrant incense, anointing oil

37.19, 20 almonds, anointing: cups made like almonds with capitals and flower

37.16, 25, 29 incense, oil, fragrant, spices: dishes for incense, altar of incense of acacia wood, fragrant incense blended, spices for anointing oil

39.38 fragrant, incense, anointing: the anointing oil

40.5, 9, 27 incense, oil, fragrant: golden altar for incense; burnt fragrant incense as Lord commanded, anointing oil to consecrate temple furniture

40.9, 10, 11, 13, 15 anoint, anointing: altar, utensils, Aaron

LEVITICUS

Leviticus is generally experienced as a dull, boring book, filled with rules and regulations. What readers need to remember is that Leviticus is reflective of how ancient Israel understood its behavior in relationship to and with God in their life of worship. Every culture develops rituals that are meaningful and important. We tend to reject/ ignore/overlook this simple fact. How will our writings, rituals, regulations appear to future generations in terms of moving the soul and the spirit?

1.9,13,17 odor: three different burnt offerings

2.2, 9 odor: cereal and burn it . . .

2.12 odor: fruit not to be burnt

2.1, 2, 5-7, 15, 16 frankincense, oil: make a cereal offering, part of cereal offering

3.5, 16 odor: peace offerings

4.7 incense, fragrant: blood on the horns of the altar of fragrant incense

4.31 odor: fat from peace offering

5.11 frankincense, oil: sin offering has no frankincense, no oil

6.15, 21 frankincense, oil, odor: cereal offering

7.10 oil: cereal offering

7.12 oil: thank offering

8.2, 10, 12, 30 oil, anointing: anointing oil

8.21 odor: ram burnt offering
8.26 bread with oil
8.28 odor: fat, etc. and bread . . .
9.4 oil: cereal offering with oil
10.1 incense: laid incense on censer, unholy fire
10.7 oil, anointing: anointing oil
14.4, 6, 49, 51, 52 cedarwood, hyssop: cleansing leprosy and leprosy in houses
14.10, 12, 15-18, 21, 24, 26-29 oil: cleansing of lepers, cereal offering with oil, log of oil, putting oil on hand, ear, for cleansing
16.12, 13 incense: offering as part of Day of Atonement
17.6 odor: peace offering
21.10, 12 oil, anointing: anointing oil makes priests holy to God
23.13 oil, odor: part of cereal offering, lamb and cereal offering
23.18 odor: seven lambs, one bull, two rams and cereal and drink offering
24.7 frankincense: frankincense goes with bread offering
26.30 incense: cut down incense altars
26.31 odors: lay waste and not smell pleasing odors

NUMBERS

Numbers is much like Leviticus, in that Numbers is not one of the books of the Bible that folks readily turn to for casual or inspirational reading. Numbers, as the name implies, is a "numbering" of the tribes of Israel, a census. Numbers also records additional laws for the Israelite nation. It is helpful to understand the breakdown of Numbers:

- Chapters 1.1-10.10 present additional laws of the law code.
- Chapters 10.11-20.13 relate Israel's journey to Kadesh and the stay in that area.
- Chapters 20.14-36.13 are the account of Israel's journey from Kadesh to Moab.

The laws that are found in Numbers concern the rights of priests and the origins of the cleansing rituals. Although the laws may seem ponderous to modern readers, for the Israelites the laws were a gift of life, since Israel understood the laws as God's instructions to govern Israel's life in the broadest sense. What the Israelites saw and experienced in the law was:

1. God is always close and caring.
2. God will always discipline.
3. God's purposes will always prevail.
4. God's love, discipline and purposes are always holy.[12]

4.7 incense: incense dish on table of bread of presence

4.16 incense, oil, fragrant, anointing: process leading up to fragrant incense, anointing oil

5.15 frankincense, oil: cereal offering of jealousy has no oil or frankincense

6.15 oil: sacrifice of flour bread with oil, wafers spread with oil

7.14, 20, 26, 32, 38, 44, 50, 56, 62, 68, 74, 80, 86 incense: part of offering from each tribal leader

7.13, 19, 25, 31, 37, 43, 49, 55, 61, 67, 73, 79 oil: cereal offering of each tribal leader has oil

8.8 oil: cereal offering

9.11 bitter herbs, which include mint

11.5 cucumber, garlic, melon, onions: murmuring in wilderness for food that is missed

11.7 bdellium, coriander: similar to description in Ex 16; manna

13.23 fig: fig trees in the land

15.3, 7, 10, 13, 14, 24 odor: burnt, drink, lamb offerings

15.4, 6, 9 oil: cereal offering

16.7, 17, 18, 35 incense: men offering incense to God; God consumes them with fire

16.40, 46, 47 incense: warning and atonement

17.8 almonds: the rod of Aaron had separated...bore ripe almonds. The significance here is that a rod which is a piece of dead wood comes to life. It is a play on words, as the Hebrew word for rod and tribe are the same. As a dead piece of wood can sprout and blossom so then can Israel be restored. Buds bring forth blossoms, which lead to ripe almonds. Aaron's rod is a reminder and a symbol of what God can and will do.[13]

18.12 oil: best of oil given as gift

18.17 odor: firstling, fat

19.6, 18 cedarwood, hyssop: purification rites

20.5 fig: complaint that land does not have figs

24.6 cedar, aloes: like aloes that the Lord has planted; like cedar trees beside the waters

28.2 odor: burnt

28.6 odor: Sinai burnt

28.8 odor: lamb

28.13 odor: flour and oil similar to cereal

28.24 odor: food of an offering

28.27 odor: two bulls, one ram, the male lambs and cereal and ...

28.5, 9, 12, 13, 20, 28 oil: cereal offering

29.2 odor: burnt

29.6 odor: spilled out

29.8 odor: burnt

29.13 odor: detailed burnt

29.36 odor: detailed burnt

29.3, 9, 14 oil: cereal offering

35.25 anointed: high priest anointed with holy oil

35.26 oil: priest anointed with holy oil

DEUTERONOMY

8.8 fig, figs: remember journey and how God has cared for the people

12.17 oil: do not eat the tithe of...oil

14.23 oil: can eat tithe...oil

18.4 oil: first fruits...oil

32.10 apple: image of that which is precious and is particularly worthy of protection (similar to Psalm 17.8 and Proverbs 7.2)

33.10 incense: part of blessing of Moses; Levites to be priests; bring incense—this implies the smoke of the sacrifices.

33.24 oil: blessing of Ashar—the idea that oil will be abundant

JOSHUA

JUDGES
9.10, 11 fig: part of a fable reflecting on the character of Abimelech
9.15 cedars: Abimelech disastrous end

RUTH
3.3 anoint: Ruth anoints self to meet Boaz

I SAMUEL
2.28 incense: call of Samuel and one task is to burn incense
9.16 anoint: anoint individual
10.1 oil: vial of oil to anoint
15.1 anoint: Samuel anoints Saul
16.3 anoint: anoint for me one who I name
16.12 anoint: arise, anoint (David)
16.13 oil, anointed: Samuel took horn of oil and anointed him
25.18 fig: she made pressed figs
30.12 fig: figs as food

II SAMUEL
5.11 cedar: construction; world is beginning to notice King David.
5.23, 24 balsam: hear the sound of marching in the balsam trees; suggests the footsteps of the Lord; when the branches move/wave, that is the sign to attack.
7.2, 7 cedar: construction

I KINGS
1.34, 39 oil, anoint, anointed: horn of oil to anoint Solomon. The horn of oil was a specific item kept in the tent that housed the ark of covenant. It was an essential part of the public act of consecration.
3.3 incense: Solomon burnt incense. Here the burning of incense by Solomon is not a good thing; he burnt incense in high places, meaning

to pagan gods.

4.25 fig: every man will have vine and fig; suggests a time of peace and contentment; compares with Deuteronomy 8.8 and Micah 4.4, which are also times of contentment.

4.33 cedar, hyssop: Solomon knew of the wood/tree. Cedar is the tallest, hyssop the smallest. Solomon is thought to have created parks and gardens in the south of Jerusalem and at Bethlehem. The passage gives an indication of the breadth of Solomon's education—standard school exercise for students of that time was to list the flora and fauna (see Proverbs 6.6-8; 26.2-3,11; 28.1, 15).[14]

5.6, 8-10 cedar/s, cypresses: construction

6.9, 10, 15, 16, 18, 20, 34, 36 cedar, cypress: temple construction

7.2, 3, 7, 11, 12 cedar: house of first hall of throne

7.50 incense: dishes for incense in temple

9.11 cedar, cypress: supplied with

9.25 incense: Solomon three times a year to bring incense. Solomon made possible, and provided, the incense for the observances at Passover, Pentecost and the Feast of Tabernacles.[15]

10.2, 10 spices: great quantity spices; probably a "trade mission," which would have included balsam and frankincense.

10.25 myrrh, spices: gifts brought to honor King Solomon

10.27 cedar: plentiful as common wood

11.8 incense: Solomon burnt incense for his foreign wives; the people are moving away from pure worship of God to corrupt or syncretistic worship.

12.33 incense: Jereboam's idolatry

13.1, 2 incense: continuation of above story

19.15, 16 anoint: various people anointed kings over Israel

22.43 incense: people still burned incense to idols

II KINGS

9.1, 3, 6 oil, anoint: pouring oil to anoint Jehu

12.3 incense: people burned incense in high places—idolatry. It is helpful to keep in mind that "high places" implies an altar to, or for, other gods.

14.4 incense: people burned incense in high places—idolatry
14.9 cedar: battle metaphor, a fable in which Jehoash is the cedar and Amaziah is the thistle.
15.4, 35 incense: people burned incense in high places—idolatry
16.4 incense: Ahaz, King of Israel, burned incense in wrong places.
17.11 incense: high places and idolatry
18.4 incense: Hezekiah's reforms. He tore down the "high places."
18.31 figs: metaphor for peace when there will be no peace
19.23 cedars, cypresses: analogy of destruction
20.7 figs: bring a cake of figs; food or perhaps poultice; presents the prophet as a healer. Poultice is a better translation than cake.
20.13 oil, spices: Hezekiah shows treasure house, which has spices and precious oil.
22.17 incense: idolatry
23.5, 8 incense: punishing priests who burned incense to idols
25.14 incense: fall of Jerusalem; temple ransacked; dishes for incense taken away

I CHRONICLES

6.49 incense: lineage of Levites; Aaron offers offering on altar, an incense for atonement.
9.29 incense, oil: genealogy of families returning; one family has oversight of oil, incense, spices.
9.29 spices: returning exiles appointed caretakers of spices; some blended them.
12.40 figs: symbol of food, peace and prosperity
14.1 cedar: trees sent
14.14-15 balsam: (repeat of 2 Sam 5)
17.1 cedar: repeat I Kings; house for God
22.4 cedar: timbers without number
23.13 incense: Aaron and sons burn incense
23.29 oil: offerings mixed with oil
28.18 incense: instruction for building temple altar of incense

II CHRONICLES

1.15 cedar: see I Kings 10.27

2.3, 8 cedar, cypress: send me these kinds of wood

2.4, 6 incense, spices: Solomon builds temple to have place to burn incense and sweet spices to God.

3.5 cypress: nave lined with

4.22 incense: dishes for incense part of temple furnishings

9.1, 9, 24 spices: Sheba brought spices to Solomon as did other kings

9.24 myrrh: similar to I Kings 10.25; gifts to honor king

9.27 cedar: similar to 1.15

13.11 incense, spices: Abijah properly offers incense of sweet spices.

14.5 incense: destruction of altar of incense for idolatry

16.14 spices: Asa died; bier filled with spices

24.14 incense: Joash restoration of temple and altar of incense

25.18 cedar: similar to 2 Kings 14.9

26.16, 18, 19 incense: Uzziah burned incense to God instead of priests doing it, so he is punished with leprosy.

28.3, 4, 25 incense: Ahaz burns incense to idols

29.7, 11 incense: improper use, proper use in temple of burning incense

30.14 incense: altar of incense

31.5 oil: first fruits...oil

32.27 spices: Hezekiah treasure of spices

34.4, 7, 25 incense: break down altar of incense to Baal, people burnt incense to idols

EZRA

3.7 cedar: rebuilding of temple—work begins in earnest after a payment is made to the workers and traders.

6.9 oil: as priests require—making sure priests have what they need to provide worship

NEHEMIAH

8.15 myrtle: make booths as it is written

10.37, 39 oil: contribution. This is all based upon the rules, laws, codes found in the Pentateuch; it is the appropriate action for a restored people and a restored temple.[16]

13.5 frankincense with cereal offering
13.5, 9 oil: tithe of...oil
13.15 figs: figs being harvested

ESTHER

2.12 myrrh, oil, spices: six months with oil and myrrh; six months with spices and ointments; period of beautifying; "in them" not applying them; utilized through fumigation or bathing

JOB

16.13 gall: he pours out my gall on the ground; "celestial archer" pierces Job and the "juices" flow; friends are supposed to bring comfort, not pain.
20.14, 25 gall: it is the gall of asps within him; evil deeds no matter how pleasurable bring ruin; gall as a poisonous substance; what the wicked eat will turn in the stomach.
24.24 mallow: men who wither and fade like mallow; what happens to the wicked
30.4 mallow: mallow as a "last ditch" food
40.17 cedar: makes tail stiff-like
40.21, 22 lotus: lotus plants...shade. These references from Chapter 40 could refer to what we call a hippopotamus today. At the very least, the image is that of a large beast (Behemoth) that lives among the thorny lotus plants.

PSALMS

17.8 apple: This references Deuteronomy 32.10, with the thought that Israel here is a "new" Israel in a new covenant; in old English, "pupil of eye" referred to a manikin, a little man, meaning that the pupil gave back a reflection of the grown man as a little man, the same imagery occurs in Hebrew. The overall intent of the verse is that God has redeemed the person.[17]
23.5 oil, anointest: anointest head with oil; evil is present in the

world but the faithful should not fear because God is there with them.
29.5 cedars: voice of God breaks; power of the voice of God. Compare with the "raw, untamed power" in Genesis 1.2; God works to overcome chaos and restore order.[18]
37.35 cedar: description of evil man. Empire and/or power of rich, evil person collapses quickly; part of a collection of sayings that speaks of deeds and consequences
45.7 oil, anointed: anointed with oil of gladness
45.8 cassia, aloes, myrrh, fragrant: ode for a wedding; robes fragrant with…This verse and the immediate preceding one describe elements of a royal wedding.
51.7 hyssop: prayer for healing and moral renewal. A model for confession, verses 7-9 are similar to verses 1-2; the psalmist is ready to do the ritual in order to be cleansed and forgiven.[19]
80.10 cedars: prayer for restoration—a theological interpretation of the exile; the people grew strong and then the people degenerated.
89.20 oil, anointed: my oil have anointed David—God found David and then anointed him. (see also II Samuel 7.4-17 and I Chronicles 17.3-15)
92.12 cedar: righteous grow like; letting thoughts be known on a Sabbath day; palm and cedar trees are mentioned; righteous person feels like a cedar tree, tall and strong.[20]
104.5 oil: part of God's blessings; colorful language describing the mystery of creation
104.16,17 cedars, fir: hymns to God. God must be glad that someone (the psalmist) loves the world so much.
105.33 figs: story of God's great deeds on behalf of people; come, seek and remember; part of the story of oppression in Exodus; the image of the plague and its harshness
133.2 oil: precious oil; in praise of brotherly love, "precious" brings to mind the alabaster box with the ointment used on Jesus in the gospels; appreciate the common joys of life and credit God because of the well ordered generosity of God.[21]
141.2 incense: let prayer be counted as incense; psalmist is at home praying and asks God to let his prayer ascend and be heard.

148.9 cedars: praise God; cosmic praise; all of creation is in worship and praise of God.

PROVERBS

5.4 wormwood: she is bitter as…part of a description of the threat of a seductive woman; wisdom is the best protection against such a woman; verses 3-14 speak of the wrong kind of woman; verses 15-19 tell of the right kind of woman.

7.2 apple: keep focused and live, actually metaphorical usage; two kinds of love, two ways of life

7.17 cinnamon, myrrh, aloes: wisdom was safeguard against adultery; all these pleasures can be enjoyed, but pay attention, youth never called wisdom his "sister," he allowed himself to be duped and seduced; this verse and the preceding notation (7.2) are part of the final lecture and warning against forbidden women. [22]

25.11 apple: Words have to have a setting in order to be heard and understood.

27.9 oil: oil and perfume make heart glad; anointing and beautiful scents gladden the heart; this is good, but a good and faithful friend is better.

27.18 fig: he who tends a fig tree will eat its fruit. Tends/guards are a "fixed pair" in the proverb—caring for a fig tree is like caring for the master; dutiful farmer eats the fruit of the tree; servant shares in the honor and prestige of the master.[23]

ECCLESIASTES

10.1 odor: give off an evil odor; a "miscellaneous" proverb; only takes a little of something bad to spoil something good[24]; ounce of folly undoes pound of wisdom; wisdom easily canceled by its opposite[25]

12.5 almond: the almond tree blossom—white hair of the aged; a description of old age; youthful vigor versus incapacitating old age; humankind and nature are closely related. (one of the toughest sections of Ecclesiastes to interpret and understand philologically[26])

SONG OF SOLOMON

Song of Solomon is also called the Song of Songs. It is a collection of 25 poems, or fragments of poems, which are presented as eight chapters in the Bible. These poems are sensuous and contain erotic imagery. There is no real, clear religious content within them; however, over the centuries, scholars have suggested the religious imagery is allegorical, if one takes the perspective of God as husband of the people, or of Christ and his love for his bride, the church. Song of Solomon overflows with the use of fragrances, oils and incense.

1.3 oil, oils, fragrant, anointing: anointing oils are fragrant—oils are integral ingredients of life's festive moments (see Ecclesiastes 9.7-8; Psalm 23.5; Proverbs 21.17); perfume often synonymous with oil and used along with spices by both women and men. Women wore cones of ointment on their heads. The cones would melt because of the warmth of the room or the warmth of the person. In melting, the cone would emit an aroma. Sweet smelling blossoms or ground resins were mixed with oil and boiled down to make the ointments. A person's fragrance stood for his/her name or reputation. (see Ecclesiastes 7.1)[27]

1.12 nard, fragrance: lover's dialogue—poem of admiration spoken by woman

1.13 myrrh: bag of myrrh between breasts. From 3,000 B.C. onward, cloth was wrapped around an item (spice, resin) and pinned to make a bag that gave off an erotic and/or sacred aroma.

1.14 henna: part of lovers' dialogue; henna believed to have life giving quality; had a pleasant aroma; often wrapped in fine linen and placed in grooves in body

1.17 cedars: pine beams of house are; cedar suggests an image more divine than royal; also possible image of the tree of life (see Ezekiel 31.6). Verses 1.16b-17 provide an interesting look at a conflict between the prophets and the people. The prophets decried the idea of making love "everywhere" as a continuation of and concession to the cultic practices of Baal. However, the people—particularly the people of the Song of Solomon—celebrate love-making here as a way to surround one's own vitality with life-giving blooming and the all-encompassing vitality of nature, which has nothing to do with Baal.[28]

2.1 rose: rose of Sharon—crocus is a more appropriate translation; KJV uses rose. The suggestion is that the woman is not a specific beauty but one beauty from among many; the word used here for rose is similar to the word used in Isaiah 25.1 for crocus; another possibility is that the flower was a sea daffodil, which was a noteworthy flower with some splendor.

2.3, 5 apple: erotic symbol, an aphrodisiac; the apple is nourishing but does not satisfy the real hunger; shadow mentioned in verse 3 implies protection with a sense of security; when the woman tastes the apple, she tastes of tenderness and the erotic attention of her lover she finds sweet.[29]

2.13 fragrance, figs: metaphor for life and hope; a song of yearning

3.6 frankincense, myrrh, fragrant: wedding procession; fragrant powders. The whole point of this section is to underscore splendor and opulence.

4.6 frankincense, myrrh: the charms of the maiden; description of the physical charms of the woman; promises of experiences of previously unknown rapture; quite erotic[30]

4.10 fragrance, spice: fragrance of oil better than spice; her own fragrance, a natural odor that she emits with perfume

4.13 henna, nard: search for lover; life-giving quality

4.14 calamus, nard, saffron, cinnamon, myrrh, aloes, frankincense, spices: description of orchard/love; fascinating imagery; lists four of the elements of the holy oil (see Exodus 30.23-24), refers to the king's garments (see Psalm 45.8), and also the harlot's bed (see Proverbs 7.17). The entire image is deliberately overwhelming and exaggerated.[31]

4.16 fragrance: wind, garden, fragrance

5.1 myrrh, spice: gather myrrh with spice

5.5, 13 myrrh, fragrance, spices: lover's appearance; cheeks like bed of spices; fragrance; description of an experience or perhaps a dream

5.15 cedars: lover's appearance—part of the woman's response to a question in 5.9, in which she describes her lover

6.2 spices: beloved gone to garden; beds of spices; beginning of woman's response to question raised in 6.1; the woman describes the pleasure that the man sees in her.

7.8 apple: admiration and yearning; heavy breathing and the scent produced by passion (similar to the scent of apples); apples are a fruit that arouses love.[32]

7.13 fragrance: mandrakes…fragrance—fragrance of mandrakes or love apples; mandrake is a fruit, *Mandragora officinarum*; the fruit, and especially its aroma, were believed to be aphrodisiacs.

8.5 apple: an image of safety and security

8.9 cedar: description of her chastity

8.14 spices: young stag upon mount of spices—image of strength of relationship, deep mutual trust and understanding

ISAIAH

1.8 cucumber, melon: part of an oracle against rebellious Judah. Shacks were built to protect the workers in the vineyards from heat, cold and damp. This is not the growing season, so the image is one of silence and loneliness; a general indictment by God over the people.

1.13 incense: oracle; incense is abomination; people are on their own without God; God will not look, listen nor attend to their worship/ offering.

2.13 cedars: day of the Lord. Even the haughty and proud, whom the world experiences as visibly impressive, strong and self sufficient, are no match against God who easily overcomes them.

6.13 terebinth: burned like…Call of Isaiah as prophet; the people do not comprehend what is happening, that Israel shall be judged and made an unhealed people until the stump remains standing.

9.10 cedars: judgment; the people refuse to recognize the trouble facing them; Israel ignores the warnings from God.

14.8 cedars, cypresses: return from exile; rejoicing over the downfall of the tyrant; trees are relieved over a new lease on life; words of rejoicing

17.8 incense: oracle against tribe/altar of incense. Israel's troubles come from looking away from God and toward the seductive alternatives.

27.9 incense: apocalyptic poem of deliverance; altars of incense destroyed—words of assurance

28.4 fig: a first ripe fig before summer; oracles on Judah and Ephraim; vision of destruction; Israel will be swallowed like a tasty fig.

28.25, 27 cummin, dill: parable of farmer; God has planned just as a farmer does—good farmers know what to do and when to do it; so does God. God knows the right time and will come with judgment and hope at the right time.

34.4 fig: from the fig tree—day vengeance; leaves fall; tree dries up; death

35.1 rose: in Kings James Version

36.16 fig: everyone his own fig tree; part of a speech by Assyrians to lure Judah into submission; peace would be just for a short while; deceiving words

37.24 cedars, cypresses: part of the mocking of Assyria and King Sennacherib (parody of words and power—I...I...I ...)

38.21 figs: take a cake of figs and apply it to the boil; healing brought about; God heals ailing nation.

39.2 oil, spices: precious oil; Hezekiah treasure of spices (similar to II Chronicles 32.24-31); Hezekiah displays treasures and wealth; he should not have done that.

41.19 cedar, cypress, myrtle, acacia, olive, pine: power of God recreating; image of a new era of well-being

43.23 frankincense: Israel ignored and offended God. Ingratitude. "Worship" is done slavishly, not with gratitude; God desires to be worshipped, and despite Israel's thoughts, the people were not worshipping.

44.14 cedar/s: parody on idol making; making fun of the seductive alternatives in the life of Israel—how difficult it is and how long it takes to craft a god, a parody.

55.13 cypress, myrtle: new exodus image. Prickly evidences of negativity are dismissed and overcome; signs of growth, life, and beauty.

57.9 oil: idolatry; idolatry and adultery; indictment; unacceptable practices continue.

60.6 frankincense: camels shall bring…When Israel is restored, there will be treasures; part of a general assurance that wealth and abundance will come in tribute to a powerful nation.

60.13 cypress, pine: similar to I Kings 5.8-10; construction

61.1 anointed: God has anointed me.

61.3 oil: oil of gladness; from powerless indebtedness to the restoration of dignity and viability

65.3, 7 incense: nature; cult practices. Israel is so unreflective and obtuse that the people cannot even recognize heavy costs. They come with bad worship habits; Israel continues to provoke God.

66.3 frankincense: memorial offering from concluding oracles; words of warning, proper obedience versus irresponsible worship.

JEREMIAH

1.11 almond: I see a rod of almond; *shaqed* vs.*shoqed* - shaqed is almond, shoqed is watching; the patient watching of God; prophet saw things others did not.

1.16 incense: incense burned to idols. Judah has done evil, and this is part of that evil; judgment against the people

5.17 figs: They shall eat up your vines and your fig trees. Consume, consume, consume—a clear theme in this section. Complete destruction; people become the fuel for the fire.[33]

6.20 frankincense: offerings not acceptable. In place of the Torah, Israel has substituted cultic practices, creating a form of religion that reflects affluence;[34] coming disaster is the fruit of people's own schemes; no amount of beautiful scents and burnt offerings could please God, who has been offended by the community's rejection of His word.[35]

8.13 figs: no grapes on the vine, nor figs on the fig tree; community is barren; it is good for nothing; picture of absolute desolation; a three-part indictment that begins in verse 11: Israel's leadership lied; there is a loss of shame; Israel is characterized as a vineyard or fig tree; the task of a plant is to produce the appropriate fruit; Israel did not produce the appropriate "fruit"; there is no connection or congruity between God's expectations and Israel's behavior.[36]

(Jeremiah 8.18 – 9.5 is one of the most powerful and pathos-filled images; nation is sick to death and sadness.)

8.22 balm: Is there no balm in Gilead? Sickness too deep, idolatry too pervasive; people refuse the necessary medicine, so no healing is possible.

9.15 wormwood: oracle; feed people wormwood—deadly potion made with poisonous herbs and fed to the people; destruction of the nation; judgment is massive and unambiguous.

10.5 cucumber: idols are like scarecrows in a cucumber field—comparison between the true God and a false god; a false god cannot do good.

11.12, 13, 17 incense: burning incense to Baal—hyperbole to show the powerlessness of gods; the people's syncretistic practices have brought destruction; harsh judgment comes when covenant is continuously violated.

17.26 frankincense: cereal offerings; remembering the Sabbath; Israel is given a choice. Will the people keep the covenant?

18.15 incense: false gods; what the nation's schemes are and what will be the consequences; Israel will follow own plan and that will bring about death (snow cannot leave the mountain and still be snow; Israel can not leave God and still be Israel, yet Israel consistently tries).[37]

19.4, 13 incense: burning incense to false gods—part of long speech of indictment against Israel. Verse 13 expands the verdict declared in verse 11. Regardless of the king's plans, God's divine intentions cancel the king's plans.

22.7, 14, 15, 23 cedar/cedars: oracles of bad omens; the high and mighty are brought down; critique of false use of power—the king has violated what it means to be king; enhances own prestige; what it means to be king and what is proper social power; community which relies upon commerce and affluence is embodied in cedars, which are doomed.[38]

23.15 cedars, wormwood: oracles of destruction—indictment, promise of judgment, poisonous herbs and water; people will be punished for their attack on prophet.

24.1-3, 5, 8 figs: vision of baskets of figs, good and bad figs; metaphor for life/death; an alternative reading of history, a reality that the prophet sees but others do not—exiled Jews/good, those in captivity God cares about vs. Jews still at home/evil.

29.17 figs:...I will make them like vile figs. People will be drawn from home and wherever exiled they shall be devastated.

32.29 incense: Baal; answer to Jeremiah's prayer; people reject God and God will respond.

34.5 spices: spices burned for ancestors; part of harsh announcement against King

41.5 incense: burning; people continue to reject God and God will respond.

44.3, 5, 8, 15, 17-19, 21, 23, 25 incense: burning incense to idols and to the "queen of heaven"; 1-14 are statements of cause/effect; 15-20 are defiant answer of the people to the prophet, we do this because it works; in 21-23, Jeremiah replies that for him God works; in 25, Jeremiah will no longer argue with the people.[39]

46.11 balm: go up to Gilead and take balm—dangerous battle; Egypt has experienced what Israel is about to experience; there is no healing.

48.35 incense: idols and incense; God's resolve is to make Moab disappear; broken like a ceramic pot.

51.8 balm: God's judgment against Babylon. In an instant, the prosperous empire falls, becomes ineffective, rhetorical, even satirical.

52.18, 19 incense: Jerusalem burned and despoiled; dishes for incense taken; loss of temple

LAMENTATIONS

3.15, 19 wormwood: sated me with wormwood—plant that yields bitter tasting medicine

3.19 gall: the wormwood and the gall—wormwood and gall appearing together creates a greater emphasis on the bitterness of the liquid.

EZEKIEL

6.4, 6 incense: altar of incense cut down because of idolatry; God had come to be seen on the same level with heathen idols; God had to share worship with the idols; Israel condemned for the practice.

6.13 odor: pleasing odor to idols. God, who is the true God, is ignored.

8.11 incense: elders burning incense, idolatry—incense offered to idols

16.9, 18, 19 oil, anointed, incense: anointed with oil, odor of unfaithfulness. Prophet's pronouncement of judgment comes in a story of an unfaithful wife, who trusted in idols.

17.3, 22, 23 cedar: allegory of eagles, and of cedar. Speaks of the house of David whose heir was Jehoachin; great tree gives protection to all of creation.

20.28 odors: sacrificed to idols; worship on the high places in Canaan.

20.41 odor: pleasing odor, accepting

23.41 incense, oil: Israel's apostasy; idolatrous incense burning

27.5 cedar, fir: good ships of Tyre built with; no skimping in selection of materials; used only the best.

27.6 pine/cypress: RSV uses pine instead of cypress, however the word may be translated cypress elsewhere in RSV.

27.17 balm, figs: a lamentation over Tyre; exchanging merchandise, which included balm, figs. This verse and the following two notations (27.19; 27.22) are part of a writing establishing Tyre's trade connections with its beauty and wealth.

27.19 calamus, cassia: bartered for merchandise

27.22 spices: the best of all kinds of spices

31.3, 8 cedar/s: allegory of cedar; description of royal power of Egypt as a magnificent tree; trees in the garden of God, "obviously" inferior to this "world tree."

45.14, 24, 25 oil: parts of offering; offerings in addition to the tithe

46.5, 7, 11, 14, 15 oil: parts of offerings; part of the offering regulations

DANIEL

2.46 incense: Nebuchadnezzar; incense offering to honor Daniel and

God—payment of homage to Daniel; reversal of role/situation—Jew so often the inferior, now the Jew is superior and God is honored; Daniel as representative of true God receives honor on behalf of God.

4.11-12, 30-31: These verses contain the dream that Jesus apparently alluded to in his parable of the mustard seed.

HOSEA

2.12 fig:…lay waste her vines and her fig trees. Israel thinks that the figs are the result of fertility rites; God passes judgment.

2.13 incense: burning incense to Baal; Israel celebrates idolatrous feast days and God will visit with punishment.

4.13 terebinth: shade is good, make offerings under them; God's beloved "bride" (Israel) turns to wooden idols for guidance. The comment about the pleasant shade is sarcasm, more than just offerings being offered there.

9.10 fig: like the first fig on the fig tree—wistful nostalgia; God remembers days before Canaan, when Israel was just as delightful as the first ripe figs. First ripe has same root as first born. Thus, this becomes a pun; fig is Israel (see Jeremiah 24.2; Matthew 21.19; Mark 11.12; Luke 13.6 where the fig tree stands for all of Israel).[40]

11.2 incense: burning incense to idols; son is prodigal; covenant relationship is broken.

14.6, 7 fragrance: reborn Israel, fragrance like Lebanon—roots go very deep; image of healing.

14.8 cypress, evergreen: God guides and sustains Israel. This is the only place in the Old Testament where God's relationship with Israel is depicted by the image of a tree—constant greenness, not diminished with changing seasons; in God alone will Israel know life.[41]

JOEL

1.7, 12 apple, fig: splintered my fig tree. Work of the locusts' teeth pictured here; implication is one of total devastation; clear why wine drinkers are first to lament; lack of harvest is a disgrace, blessing has been withdrawn.

2.22 fig: tree bears its fruit; the fig tree. An assurance oracle in response to plea in 1.16-20.

AMOS

2.9 cedars: destroyed...height like cedars; totality and finality of destruction

4.9 fig: your fig trees and your olive trees the locust devoured; increasing severity (not just the usual crop failure but the unexpected); catalogue of calamity; disasters come because of God's doing.

5.7 wormwood: turn justice to wormwood. Israel's unwillingness to repent and return, bitterness of calamity; justice in creatures has been changed by greed to a bitter calamity; justice has been perverted.

6.6 oils, anoint: anointed with oils, woe...anoint selves with finest oils. Instead of following ancient tradition of dedicating best of one's possessions to God, people chose to enhance selves through luxury; opulent feasting by the upper class who are so self centered and intent on own pleasure that they find Amos' predictions of catastrophe incredible; no concern for thè breakdown of the community.[42]

6.12 wormwood: fruit of righteousness turned to wormwood. People are overturning the concept of justice; displays the incredible nature of what is happening in Israel; the absurd is happening; injustice among the poor in the courts.

OBADIAH

JONAH

MICAH

4.4 fig: under his vine and under his fig tree; quality of peace, ideal situation for farmer freed from threats of the military state.

6.7 oil: Will the Lord be pleased...with ten thousands of rivers of oil? What will please the Lord? A series of escalations? First born?

6.15 anoint: but not anoint with oil. Blessings become curses; fertility becomes means of bitter frustration.

7.1 fig: no first ripe fig, which my soul desires. Opening cry of anguish; hungry person in the midst of harvested grove or vineyard.

NAHUM

3.12 fig: All your fortresses are like fig trees with first-ripe figs. Nineveh, a stronghold, will fall easily just as when you shake a tree with ripe fruit the fruit falls easily; or fruit falls with a strong wind; ripe for the taking.

HABBAKUK

1.16 incense: profane worship. Fishing metaphor. Do we deify our own means to a high standard of living? Babylonian worshipers' tools are used to reap abundance.

3.17 fig: Though the fig trees do not blossom—Habakkuk's decision to wait patiently for fulfillment of vision, come what may. Even if outward signs point to God's absence, Habakkuk will not lose hope.

ZEPHANIAH

2.14 cedar: judgment and wood laid bare—elaborate description of ruined city.[43]

HAGGAI

2.19 fig: God blesses...do the vine, the fig tree, the pomegranate...Technical form in which a question is put to a prophet—what does the future hold? Blessings will come. Questions refer to verses 2.16 and 2.17.

ZECHARIAH

1.8, 10, 11 myrtle: standing among myrtle trees—symbol of happiness, which implies a state of rest, soon to come or has arrived; myrtle tree was a hardy shrub usually found in dense growth; bright green leaves.

2.8 apple: image reflected; to touch Judah is to touch God; anyone who acts injuriously to Israel does the same thing to God, or toward one of the most sensitive and important parts of God's being.

11.1, 2 cedar/s, cypress: fall of tyrants; gracious, aristocratic trees, symbol of worldly pride; fear divine judgment because know judgment is coming.

MALACHI

1.11 incense: offering incense to God; worship anywhere, can do proper ritual outside of Jerusalem and even outside of Israel. Whether or not appropriate ritual is done in Jerusalem, God's name will be praised appropriately somewhere else.

MATTHEW

2.11 frankincense, myrrh: gift of magi; royal gifts; myrrh described by one commentary as a resin of an Arabian shrub with a pleasant aroma.

6.17 anoint: when fast, anoint head, wash face—faith in action versus mere religious activity.

7.16 figs: Are your grapes gathered from thorns or figs from thistles? A tree can only produce appropriate fruit, i.e., a bad tree cannot produce good fruit; beware of false prophets who try to produce "good fruit" but can't; actions are characteristic of inner person.

13.31 mustard: The kingdom of heaven is like a grain of mustard seed; insignificant beginning, magnificent end.

17.20 mustard: If you have faith as a grain of mustard seed ... Disciples have faith in Jesus, but their faith becomes endangered when they confront overwhelming challenges; the goal is true faith, not little faith.

21.19-21 fig: fig tree cursed. Important to read this passage in the context of Matthew 22.11-14 which talks about time of the coming of the son of man as when "fruits" are to be produced; another emphasis upon faith; strong faith can work wonders.

23.23 cummin, dill, mint: tithe but...Pharisees do not recognize justice, mercy, faithfulness as the weightier matters of law; they devote selves to fulfilling minor issues; important to remember all aspects of the law.

24.32 fig: From the fig tree learn its lesson. Watch for the signs ...

26.6-13: (Matthew's nard/ointment narrative) addressed under "nard" in the main text.

27.34 gall: They offered him wine to drink, mingled with gall—a mocking of Jesus. Gall is a bad drink, more humiliation and embarrassment; Jesus submits to the suffering.

MARK

4.31 mustard: It is like a grain of mustard seed—epitome of smallness; difficult for followers to comprehend ultimate reign of God that begins so small.

6:13 oil, anointed: disciples anointed others with oil. The disciples extended the work of Jesus by the authority of Jesus; oil often used as a medicament. Here the oil/healing is a spiritual symbol but is used effectively because it is recognized as a medicament as well.

11.13, 20, 21 fig: fig tree cursed. May refer to small buds, which were considered "delicacies." These became ripe when leaves appeared. Image is that of God coming to temple to find spiritual fruit and none was there[44]; Jesus looking for edible fruit and found only leaves also suggests Israel's outward show of religion and failure to produce anything of worth.

13.28 fig: from the fig tree learn its lesson; "general countryman's parable"[45]; ties in with previous parable; fig tree one of the most common trees in Palestine, harbinger of summer; hope and not destruction is the final word.

14.3, 8 nard, anointed: woman has anointed my body with jar of nard—nard a highly valued Indian plant according to one commentary. The image is that the gift is "total" giving; ointment jars for the anointing of the dead were often broken and left in the tomb.[46]

15.23 myrrh: Jesus drank myrrh. Offer of a pain killing drink; would have been offered by Jewish sympathizers, probably pious/faithful women; this would not have been offered by the executioners.

16.1 spices, anoint: Mary Magdalene, Mary, Salome...anoint... spices for Jesus' body. The women try to do what was not possible to do at the time of the burial; an act of ultimate devotion, especially given that a most unpleasant odor would be present after 36 hours in the tomb; women still unable to complete the act of devotion because of the resurrection; perfumed ointments suggests an ointment or oil and not dry materials, and this agrees with the general Jewish tradition.[47]

LUKE

1.9-11 incense: Zechariah burning incense properly. Priest presses bowl of incense down on the coals in the holy place behind the outer curtain; this is done twice daily—in the morning before the burnt offering in the outer court, and in the afternoon around 3:00 when a large crowd is gathered; when people saw smoke rising, a sign of consecration to God, they would bow down and pray silently; there were so many priests that only once in a lifetime did a priest get to do this offering.

4.18 anointed: Jesus reads Isaiah 61.1, which uses *anointed*

6.44 fig: figs are not gathered from thorns. Similar to Matthew 7.16, as a person is within his/her own deepest being so will the person act; an indestructible law of nature.[48]

7.38, 46 oil, anoint, anointed: did not anoint head with oil but she did anoint feet....Simon calls Jesus to his home out of curiosity, the woman comes to the home out of love; abundant love is not the cause of forgiveness but the result of forgiveness.

7.36-50: encompasses the above verses. Luke's version of the nard/ointment narrative. Narrative shows Jesus' openness to those who stand on, or beyond, the fringes of the people of God; the narrative carries an additional warning against self sufficiency, thinking that one stands in need of nothing; healing does take place, the healing from meaninglessness in life (release from).[49]

10.34 oil: Good Samaritan bound up wounds with oil and wine; act of medical healing, act of love.

11.42 mint, rue: You tithe mint and rue and every herb and neglect justice....Religious leaders amazingly particular in giving tithes, but neglect the call of the law for true justice and righteousness toward people and love for God.

13.6, 7 fig: I have come seeking fruit on this fig tree. Three-year standard probationary period for the vineyard has ended; vineyard dresser asks for one more year in which to provide special care; if nothing grows, if change does not occur, then vineyard will be destroyed. God has given Israel plenty of time to bear fruit, but God will give one more chance. ... [50] (see Isaiah 5.1-7; Hosea 9.10; Micah 7.1; Jeremiah 8.13, where Israel is symbolized as fig or vineyard)[51]

13.19 mustard: It is like a grain of mustard seed. Similar to Matthew 13 and Mark 4. God's realm appears in Jesus the "humiliated" but will grow quickly and irresistibly to a vast movement.

17.6 mustard: If you had faith as a grain of mustard seed. Similar to Matthew 17.20, Pharisees dependent upon the continuing validity of the law; disciples are dependent upon faith, which they pray for as a gift; mustard seed does contain the germ of life and that is all that is needed; disciples need faith of the same quality and vigor.

21.29 fig: Look at the fig tree. Similar to Mark 13.28-32. With a short introduction the parable becomes a universal law of nature.

23.56 spices: Women prepared spices for body; obedience to the commandments; women not hesitant to serve regardless of the cost.

24.1 spices: took spices; the women had made the preparation, now they could go and do.

JOHN

1.48, 50 fig: when you were under the fig tree. Fig tree is a symbol of home (see Isaiah 36.16; Micah 4.4; Zechariah 3.10), a place for prayer, meditation and study; Nathanael had experience of communion with God that Jesus recognized[52]; some rabbis taught law under fig trees; Nathanael seen as a pious Jew.[53]

9.6,11 anointed: anointed man's eye with the clay; spittle contains curative properties, or so it was believed, and is used to make an ointment. Perhaps it is also a reflection of Genesis 2.7.

11.2 anointed: references action of John 12.3—an "explanatory parenthesis" anticipating John 12.1-8; John identifies Mary as the woman who does the anointing of Jesus with the nard; this suggests that the event/narrative was well known in the early church and people would recognize the reference.

12.3 nard, fragrance, anointed: Mary anointed Jesus. 12 ounces, or about a half pint of material, oil from an aromatic plant; use of unguents for festivities in the first century very probable; not a healing preparation but a scented oil poured on head as part of festivity; Rabbinic saying: *[The scent of] good oil is diffused from the bedchamber to the dining-hall, while a good name is diffused from one end of the world to the other.* If this is what John had in mind (Mark 14.9 and John 12.3b), then the world would know of the act.[54]

19.29 hyssop: sponge full of vinegar on a hyssop (Jesus on the cross). Difficulty exists because the hyssop plant is unsuitable for this particular purpose; maybe an attempt to tie in with Exodus 12.13ff, or simply a misreading/misprinting of the Greek word for javelin[55]. Hyssop is good for sprinkling, but not for the purpose mentioned here. Yet in a crucifixion, the condemned's feet were just off the ground so a person with height could reach the lips of the condemned. Therefore, hyssop may have been used, or perhaps John simply wants to present Jesus as the perfect Passover sacrifice (Exodus 12.22).[56]

19.39 myrrh, aloes: Nicodemus made mixture for Jesus' body; herbs or crystals of the resins or gum from two aromatic plants in a dry, not liquid, form; 100 pounds would be an exaggeration but the implication is that this is a royal burial.[57] Only place in the New Testament where aloes is mentioned; John seems to want to reflect the flavor of Psalm 45.8; on the amount, see II Chronicles 16.14; John reminds the reader of Jesus' kingship and/or Nicodemus is trying to make some reparation in death for what he failed to do in life; the disciples run while Josephus and Nicodemus come out publically.[58]

19.40 spices: bound it in linen cloths with spices. John seems to suggest that these are dry materials, which would have been sprinkled between the linen cloths rather than used to anoint the body.[59]

ACTS

4.27 anoint: Jesus whom thou didst anoint

8.23 gall: For I see you are in the gall of bitterness. Echoes Deuteronomy 29.18; refers to the danger of a root springing up that bears poisons and bitter fruit, a metaphor for a person whose idolatry and godlessness lead to bitter results for the individual and for the people the individual deceives. The implication is that Simon is causing bitter judgment for himself.[60]

ROMANS

I CORINTHIANS

II CORINTHIANS

2.14, 16 fragrance: fragrance of the knowledge of Christ; fragrance death to death, life to life. Imagery comes from the environment. Roman victory parades were both political and religious, and parades would end at a temple where sacrifices were offered. The odor of such sacrifices was fragrant; the faithful should spread the fragrant aroma of the knowledge of Christ for the aroma of Christ is a sacrifice pleasing to God.[61]

The word *fragrance* in this passage, *fragrant* in Ephesians 5.2 and in Philippians 4.18, and the word for *ointment* in John 12.3 are all the same Greek word. The Greek word is actually a "neutral" word, but the setting of each occurrence implies good or sweet.[62]

2.15 aroma: aroma of Christ to God—figurative language suggesting the sweet smell of burnt offerings to God.

GALATIANS

EPHESIANS

5.2 fragrant: Christ gave self up as fragrant offering—sweet smelling savor from ancient practice and belief that God enjoyed the smell of burnt offerings (see Genesis 8.21); way to describe something believed to be pleasing to God.

(See also the above comment under II Corinthians on fragrance)

PHILIPPIANS

4.18 fragrant: offering. Offering or gift is an odor of a sweet smell (see Genesis 8.21; Exodus 2.9, 18; Leviticus 1.9, 13; Ezekiel 20.41).

Paul acknowledges a gift, and in doing so caps off a commercial metaphor that he used in 4.15, 17; brings in Old Testament imagery of a fragrant offering that is also an acceptable sacrifice.[63] (See also earlier note under II Corinthians on the use of fragrance/fragrant.)

COLOSSIANS

I THESSALONIANS

II THESSALONIANS

I TIMOTHY

II TIMOTHY

TITUS

PHILEMON

HEBREWS

1.9 oil, anointed: Anointed with oil of gladness references Psalm 45.6-7—symbol of richness and prosperity; comparison of kings who are rulers of other nations (Psalm 45.6-7) and the angels mentioned here, who are the Son's companions. They do God's will.

9.4 incense: refers to golden altar of incense of Hebrew people (see I Kings 6.20,22); reference to altar, one could never enter the inner sanctuary without incense from the altar.

9.19 hyssop: blood of calves and goats, with water and scarlet wool and hyssop and sprinkled...—an ancient custom aimed only at outward perfection (see Leviticus 14.4-9; Numbers 19.6-8; Exodus 12.22).

JAMES

3.12 fig: Can a fig tree...yield olives or a grapevine figs? In nature all things are interrelated and depend upon each other; humans should not be amazed when something does what it is supposed to do; however, what is so abundantly true and common in nature is not so with the human tongue; human tongue does not always produce what it is meant to produce, as the tongue is sometimes loyal and sometimes treacherous.

5.14 oil, anointing: anointing sick with oil—creates an image of healing, especially in that oil was a medicinal; however, the name of the Lord is invoked, therefore the oil is not the mendicant, as the healing is done by prayer.

I PETER

II PETER

I JOHN

II JOHN

III JOHN

JUDE

REVELATION

3.18 anoint: anoint eyes that you may see—warning written to Laodicea, which was noted for medical college and for Phrygian powder used to make eye salve. Phrygian physicians might aid people in physical blindness, but only Christ can heal the eyes of the spiritually blind.[64]

5.8 incense: prayers are joined with incense—censures represent the prayers of the saints.

6.13 fig: as the fig tree sheds its winter fruit; humans must face God and the consequences of their deeds, based upon Old Testament imagery; uses strident apocalyptic words (see Isaiah 13.9 ff.; 2.10 ff.; 34.4; Ezekiel 32.7ff.; 38.19; Hosea 10.8; Joel 2.10, 30ff.; Amos 8.8).[65]

8.3, 4 incense: prayers, incense, smoke; smoke of incense rises with the prayers of the saints, adding a fragrance to the prayers. God's judgment will come upon the world in answer to the prayers of the saints; prayers of the saints for justice and vindication are answered by God's fire of judgment.

8.11 wormwood: star of…and water is…The word *wormwood* occurs nowhere else in the Greek Bible. In Jeremiah 9.15, wormwood is a sign of divine judgment. Wormwood mixed with water is not a deadly poison but here there is a deadly element;[66] human actions, which may seem merely physical, have a spiritual significance and impact; what seems like a good plan or project may not, in fact, bring justice for all and/or may have humanity tampering with nature.[67]

18:13 cinnamon, frankincense, myrrh, incense, oil, spice: During war, city falls and trade is no more possible; list of merchandise for which there are no longer any buyers—most of these items also are listed in the dirge over Tyre in Ezekiel 27.5-24 (see also Ezekiel 16.9-13). The lists include precious stones, fine raiment, costly articles of decoration, fragrances, foods, beasts and slaves, and reflects the luxury and opulence of the wealthy city dwellers.[68]

Appendix 5
Glossary of Terms

Abortifacient	agent that can cause a miscarriage or likely to induce an abortion
Allopathy	system of medicine that uses drugs with effects opposite to the symptoms produced by the disease (in contrast with homeopathy)
Alterative	similar to a tonic (see below), hastening renewal and healing; restores health rather than maintaining it
Amenorrhea	absence of menstruation outside of pregnancy
Analgesic	agent that allays pain
Anesthetic	causes nerve endings to lose sensation, making less aware of pain
Anaphrodisiac	diminishing sexual drive
Anthelmintic	destroying intestinal/parasitic worms
Anti-catarrhal	stops the excessive secretion of mucus

Anti-emetic	generally carminatives and stomachics, alleviating nausea and stopping a siege of vomiting
Antifungal	not conducive to fungus
Anti-infectious	substance that tends to reduce the infectious response
Anti-inflammatory	reduces the manifestation of pain, heat, swelling and redness
Antiphlogistic	(see antipyretic)
Antipyretic	reducing inflammation or fever
Antiseptic	inhibits the growth of bacteria on wound or sore; prevents infection
Antispasmodic	calms muscles, stops spasms and convulsions
Antisudorific	reduces perspiration
Antitussive	relieving or preventing coughing
Aperient	mildly laxative
Aphrodisiac	increases sexual inclination or function
Aromatherapy	using essential oils (the volatile oil of a plant) to promote beauty, health, well being; therapeutic use of essential oils by inhalation or application to treat mental, emotional, and/or physical conditions

Aromatic	having pleasant fragrance; usually added to mixture to enhance palatability
Astringent	contracting bodily tissues; causing contraction of tissues (often mucous membranes); reducing hemorrhages, secretions, diarrhea
Calmative	mildly sedative
Cardiotonic	having a tonic effect on the heart
Carminative	relieving flatulence (wind), mild cramps and tension
Carrier oil	a basic oil, usually vegetable oil
Cathartic	strongly laxative
Cholagogic	stimulating gall bladder contraction to promote flow of bile
Cicatrisant	healing, promoting scar-tissue formation
Concoction	the result from mixing of a variety of material
Cytophylactic	encouraging cell regeneration
Cytotoxic	interfering with metabolism and replication of DNA
Decoction	herbal preparation made by boiling an herb (generally a bark, root, or seed) in a covered enamel or otherwise nonmetallic container

of water for fifteen minutes or longer

Demonofugue	old term for herb thought to expel evil spirits
Demulcent	an herb which, when ingested, lubricates and coats the stomach and intestine linings
Diaphoretic	perspiration producing; used in mild fevers, generally not as strong as a sudorific
Digestive	aids the digestion
Diuretic	stimulating the secretion of urine
Dyspepsia	disturbed digestion
Elixir	distillation or tincture
Emetic	causing vomiting
Emmenagogue	inducing, stimulating, or regularizing menstruation
Emollient	used externally for soothing, softening properties
Emulsion	fluid formed by the suspension of one liquid in another
Erethism	abnormal irritability or sensitivity
Expectorant	aids removal of catarrh; ability to loosen accumulation of phlegm in lungs, sinus cavities, or in bronchial passages

Febrifuge	helps to dispel fever, reducing temperature; antipyretic
Fixative	substance added to a perfume blend to absorb and preserve more fugitive scents
Hepatic	tonic to the liver
Homeopathy	system of medicine using tiny amounts of drugs/herbs, which in a healthy body would produce symptoms similar to those of the disease (opposite of allopathy)
Hypertension	high blood pressure
Hypertensive	that which raises blood pressure
Hypotension	low blood pressure
Hypotensive	lowers blood pressure
Infusion	strong herbal tea
Irritant	that which irritates skin
Kyphi (Cyphi)	sacred incense used in Egyptian temples
Laxative	loosens the bowel; promotes evacuation; also referred to as aperient
Liplytic	breaks down fat
Macrobiotic	a diet or practice that tends to prolong life
Mucolytic	breaks down mucus

Naturopathy	a system of treating illnesses, body upsets, etc. through natural means such as food, vitamins, air, sunshine
Nervine	helps strengthen the nerves; calming to nerves and soothing to emotions
Neurotoxic	having a destructive or toxic effect to the nervous system
Pectoral	working directly upon the lungs and chest; effective in treating congestion
Poultice	a soft, hot, moist mass of herbs/paste/meal, etc. applied to sores or inflamed parts of the body
Pulmonary	interchangeable with pectoral
Purgative	causes evacuation of the bowels; strongly laxative
Rubefacient	increases local circulation, making skin red
Sedative	producing a calming effect, tranquilizing
Simples	an herbal preparation or a "pharmaceutical recipe" for a curative
Stimulant	having a rousing, uplifting effect on body and mind
Stomachic	aiding the stomach when struggling with poor digestion and/or disorders arising from tension

Sudorific	inducing perspiration, stronger than diaphoretics
Theophany	an appearance of God or a god to humankind
Tonic	herb that stimulates some part of the body, providing nutrition to some part of the body
Vermifuge	worm expellant
Vulnerary	healing agent for cuts, wounds and sores; styptic, often antiseptic

This Glossary is a combination and adaptation of glossaries from:

Beyerl, Paul, *The Master Book of Herbalism*

Huson, Paul, *Mastering Herbalism*

Price, Shirley, *Aromatherapy Workbook: Understanding Essential Oils from Plant to Bottle*

Price, Shirley and Len Price, *Aromatherapy for Health Professionals*

Rose, Jeanne, *375 Essential Oils and Hydrosols*

Tisserand, Robert and Tony Balacs, *Essential Oil Safety: a Guide for Health Care Professionals*

A Closing Personal Reflection

"And God saw that it was good," the refrain from Genesis 1; the plain yet powerful words of Ecclesiasticus 38.2a,4: "...healing comes from the Most High....The Lord created medicines from the earth, and a sensible man will not despise them"; and the comforting words from Revelation 22.2c: "...and the leaves of the tree were for the healing of the nations. ..." speak deeply to the heart and soul. God provides for God's children regardless of the "child's" age. Humanity does itself a disservice when it chooses to ignore the wealth of healing provided by God in and through nature and creation. God the omnipotent, beneficent Healer, does provide.

Ultimately, healing is what God is all about. Jesus, in his life and ministry, clearly demonstrated the importance of healing and wholeness in and for the lives of all of God's children.

During the time that I worked on revisions of this manuscript, I received the occasional newsletter from a hospital volunteer chaplains association. Within its pages, I found this:

A Short 'History" of Medicine
"Doctor, I have an earache."

- 2000B.C. "Here, eat this root."
- 1000B.C. "That root is heathen, say this prayer."
- 1850A.D. "That prayer is superstition, drink this potion."
- 1940A.D. "That potion is snake oil, swallow this pill."
- 1985A.D. "That pill is ineffective, take this antibiotic."
- 2000A.D. "That antibiotic is artificial. Here, eat this root!"

I think again of Wilma Paterson's suggestion that in spite of all we glean from scripture concerning the use and efficacy of plants, we are not blessed with a full spectrum of knowledge concerning plant qualities and powers as used and experienced in the Biblical times. This is because the Biblical writers were concerned that to mention such things in the scriptures would be to distract from people's belief in God's all-embracing, divine power. I wonder what knowledge has been lost to the ages?

In pondering, I also consider John 20.30, "Now Jesus did many other signs in the presence of the disciples, which are not written in this book; but these are written that you may believe that Jesus is the Christ, the Son of God, and that believing, you may have life in his name"; and John 21.25, "But there are also many other things which Jesus did; were every one of them to be written, I suppose that the world itself could not contain the books that would be written." There is clear precedent for writing just enough, and not too much, so that people might believe without skepticism, which might happen if the claims and stories appeared too incredible.

I know that some religious scholars/writers and some pastors decry aromatherapy, homeopathy and naturopathy as being pagan in origin and therefore unacceptable practices for Christians. Such criticism saddens me.

Pragmatically, all knowledge has its ultimate roots in ancient cultures and some of those cultures have come to be labeled as pagan. Whether we consider public, private, or parochial schools, I think we will find that these institutions continue to use and teach the properties of mathematics even though, the "father of mathematics" is the Greek Pythagorus, a "pagan" who lived and worked around 500 B.C. Babylonian and Egyptian cultures of 3000 B.C. show indications of using basic geometric principles in their buildings. Euclid, a Greek "pagan" from around 300 B.C. is called the "father of geometry." In spite of such pagan heritage, math and geometry continue to be taught, and their truths and principles shape our lives and our cultures.

We don't eschew writing and reading, even though we can trace the genealogy of the letters we use in our alphabet back to ancient Egyptian, Semitic, Phoenician and Greek cultures with our actual current style of letters emerging from the pagan Roman culture. As outlined in Chapter 3, "God, Healing and Humankind", medicine traces its lineage to Hippocrates, a Greek. How can the assertion be made that allopathic medicine is acceptable but homeopathic is not because the latter arises from pagan cultures and practices? We turn to the scriptures and to the work of archaeologists and historians to discern the practices of our faith-ancestors, and we learn that they trusted in the words of scripture, trusted that God provided for healing.

This book is not intended as a treatise for homeopathy at the expense of allopathy. In my family, we judiciously utilize both approaches. We recognize that, from our perspective, certain conditions absolutely demand allopathic measures. We also recognize that many conditions are better addressed through homeopathy and that homeopathy works to maintain wellness. When we seek health care providers, we go to those who are open to utilizing/combining homeopathy and allopathy.

The health care that an individual or family receives is heavily influenced by geography. The range and extent of allopathic help and care available for those who live in or near metropolitan areas can differ greatly from that which is available in isolated rural communities. Family income and health benefits, if any, influence choices regarding medical care. In some nations and/or continents, people automatically turn to homeopathic care. If that does not bring healing, then—and only then—will these folks contact allopathic practitioners, provided such care is available. What we refer to in the United States as non-conventional medicine, or alternative medicine, is actually called traditional medicine in much of the world. Similarly, that which we label traditional medicine in our nation is viewed otherwise in other lands.

Wisdom literature in the scripture (Job, Psalms, Proverbs, Ecclesiastes, Song of Solomon, and parts of the prophetic writings) extols the virtue of growing in knowledge that one might grow closer to God. All of life is a journey, of course, and a vital part of that journey is to grow continually in our wisdom and knowledge of God. An aspect of our growth in knowledge is manifested in the development and advancement in medical science over the centuries. That journey also has lead us in curious circles from time to time, when we find ourselves saying, "Let's look again at what the ancients did, what our ancestors did." And when we do, we discover amazing insights into their curatives.

We trace the use of plants in the scripture and marvel at some of the similar uses that continue today. Refrains echo once again:

- God saw that it was good.
- Healing comes from the Most High.
- The Lord created medicines from the earth, and a sensible [person] will not despise them.
- The leaves of the tree are for the healing of the nations.

God has provided richly for our health and well-being. I would never forsake allopathy completely, nor will I neglect homeopathy. Trusting in the truth of the scriptures and the promises of God, I believe that God intends for humanity to utilize both allopathy and homeopathy. In doing so, we truly accept and acknowledge all that God has created and provided for us.

Aromatherapy is not new. Homeopathy is not new. Naturopathy is not new. Although not known by such names, these have existed since the beginning of time. It is my hope that this book will not only strengthen the journey already begun by so many, but that it also will give encouragement to others to venture into the world of aromatherapy, homeopathy and naturopathy for the health and well being of themselves, their loved ones, families and friends. These methodologies are grounded in scripture and are among God's gifts to us.

Endnotes

1. Laurence A. Turner, *Genesis*, (Sheffield, England: Sheffield Academic Press, 2000) p. 114

2. Turner, op. cit., p. 31

3. Gerhard von Rad, *Genesis: a Commentary*, (Philadelphia: Westminster Press, 1972) p. 31

4. von Rad, op. cit., p. 91

5. von Rad, op. cit., p. 122

6. von Rad, op. cit., p. 163

7. von Rad, op. cit., p. 184

8. Brevard S. Childs, *The Book of Exodus, a Critical and Theological Commentary*, (Louisville: the Westminster Press, 1974) p. 65

9. Childs, op. cit., p. 291

10. J. Gerald Janzen, *Exodus*, (Louisville: Westminster/John Knox Press, 1997) p. 201

11. Childs, op. cit., p. 541

12. Walter Riggans, *Numbers – the Daily Study Bible, Old Testament*, (Philadelphia: Westminster Press, 1983) pp. 2-3

13. Riggans, op. cit., pp. 138-140

14. Donald J. Wiseman, *1 and 2 Kings: an Introduction and Commentary*, (Downers Grove, Illinois: Inter Varsity Press, 1993) pp. 96-97

15. Wiseman, op. cit., p. 128

16. R.J. Coggins, *The Books of Ezra and Nehemiah*, (New York: Cambridge University Press, 1976) pp. 122-124

17. George A.F. Knight, *Psalms – the Daily Study Bible, volumes 1 and 2*, (Philadelphia: Westminster Press, 1981) p. 81

18. Walter Brueggemann, *The Message of the Psalms: a Theological Commentary*, (Minneapolis: Augsburg, 1984) p. 143

19. Brueggemann, *Psalms*, op. cit., p. 100

20. Knight, *Psalms*, op. cit., p. 99

21. Brueggemann, *Psalms*, op. cit., p. 48

22. Richard J. Clifford, *Proverbs: A Commentary*, (Louisville: Westminster/John Knox Press, 1999) pp. 84, 90

23. Clifford, op. cit., p. 239

24. Tremper Longman, III, *The Book of Ecclesiastes*, (Grand Rapids, Michigan: William B. Eerdmans Publishing Company, 1998) p. 239

25.   James L. Crenshaw, *Ecclesiastes: a Commentary*, (Philadelphia: Westminster Press, 1987) p. 169

26.   Longman, op. cit., pp. 271-272

27.   Othmar Keel, *The Song of Songs: a Continental Commentary*, (Minneapolis: Fortress Press, 1994) p. 62

28.   Keel, op. cit., p. 75

29.   Keel, op. cit., p. 82

30.   Keel, op. cit., p. 153

31.   Keel, op. cit., p. 180

32.   Keel, op. cit., pp. 246-247

33.   Walter Brueggemann, *A Commentary on Jeremiah: Exile and Homecoming*, (Grand Rapids, Michigan: William B. Eerdmans Publishing Company) p. 66

34.   Brueggemann, *Jeremiah*, op. cit., p. 74

35.   Robert P. Carroll, *Jeremiah: a Commentary*, (Philadelphia: The Westminster Press, 1986) p. 201

36.   Brueggemann, *Jeremiah*, op. cit., pp. 89-90

37.   Brueggemann, *Jeremiah*, op. cit., p. 170

38.   Brueggemann, *Jeremiah*, op. cit., pp. 200, 203

39.   Brueggemann, *Jeremiah*, op. cit., pp. 407-408

40. George A.F. Knight, *Hosea*, (London: SCM Press, 1960) p.85

41. James Luther Mays, *Hosea: a Commentary*, (London: SCM Press, 1969) pp. 189-190

42. James Luther Mays, *Amos: a Commentary*, (London: SCM Press, 1969) p. 120

43. J.J.M. Roberts, *Nahum Habakkuk, and Zephaniah: a Commentary*, (Louisville: Westminster/John Knox Press, 1991) p. 157

44. The Rev. Canon R.A. Cole, *The Gospel According to Mark: an Introduction and Commentary*, (Grand Rapids, Michigan: William B. Eerdmans Publishing Company, 1989) pp. 250-251

45. Cole, op. cit., p. 281

46. Morna Hooker, *The Gospel According to Saint Mark*, (London: Hendrickson Publishing Incorporated, 1991) pp. 328-330

47. Leon Morris, *The Gospel According to John: the English Text with Introduction, Exposition and Notes*, (Grand Rapids, Michigan: William B. Eerdmans Publishing Company, 1971) p. 593

48. Norval Geldenhuys, *Commentary on the Gospel of Luke: the English Text with Introduction, Exposition and Notes*, (Grand Rapids, Michigan: William B. Eerdmans Publishing Company, 1977) p. 214

49. Eduard Schweizer, *The Good News According to Luke*,

(Atlanta: John Knox Press, 1984) pp.139-141

50.   Geldenhuys, op. cit., p. 372

51.   Schweizer, *Luke*, op. cit., p. 220

52.   Morris, op. cit., p. 167

53.   Barnabas, editor, *The Gospel of John*, (London: Oliphants, 1972) p. 118

54.   Morris, op. cit., pp. 576-577

55.   Lindars, op. cit., pp. 581-582

56.   Morris, op. cit., pp. 813-814

57.   Lindars, op. cit., p. 592

58.   Morris, op. cit., pp. 825-826

59.   Lindars, op. cit., p. 592

60.   I. Howard Marshall, *The Acts of the Apostles: an Introduction and Commentary*, (Grand Rapids, Michigan: William B. Eerdmans Publishing Company, 1998) p. 159

61.   Simon J. Kestemaker, *Exposition of the Second Epistle to the Corinthians*, (Grand Rapids, Michigan: William B. Eerdmans Publishing Company, 1997) p. 90

62.   Roger L. Omanson and John Ellengton, *Paul's Second Letter to the Corinthians*, (New York: United Bible Society Handbook Series, 1993) p. 50

63. Gordon D. Fee, *Paul's Letter to the Philippians*, (Grand Rapids, Michigan: William B. Eerdmans Publishing Company, 1995) pp. 450-451

64. George Eldon Ladd, *A Commentary on the Revelation of John*, (Grand Rapids, Michigan: William B. Eerdmans Publishing Company, 1972) p. 66

65. Marcus Maxwell, *Revelation*, (New York: Doubleday, 1998) p. 55

66. Ladd, op. cit., p. 127

67. Maxwell, op. cit., p. 73

68. Ladd, op. cit., p 230

Bibliography

Ackerknecht, Erwin H., *A Short History of Medicine*, New York: The Ronald Press, Company, 1955

Alden, Robert, *Job, volume II, the New American Commentary*, Nashville: Broadman and Holman Publishers, 1993

Apocrypha and Pseudepigrapha of the Old Testament in English with Introductory and Critical Explanatory Notes to the Several Books, The, volume 2 – the Pseudepigrapha, R.H. Charles, ed., Oxford, Clarendon, 1913/1979

Attridge, Harold W., *A Commentary on the Epistle to the Hebrews*, Philadelphia: Fortress Press, 1989

Barclay, William, *The Daily Study Bible: the Gospel of Mark*, Edinburgh: The Saint Andrew Press, 1962

Barclay, William, *The Daily Study Bible: the Revelation of John, volume 2*, Philadelphia: The Westminster Press, 1976

Berdoe, Edward, *The Origin and Growth of the Healing Art: a Popular History of Medicine in all Ages and Countries*, London: Swan Sonnenschein and Company, 1893

Beyerl, Paul, *The Master Book of Herbalism*, Custer, Washington: Phoenix Publishing Company, 1984

Brueggemann, Walter, *A Commentary on Jeremiah: Exile and Homecoming*; Grand Rapids, Michigan: William B. Eerdmans, Publishing Company, 1998

Brueggemann, Walter, *Isaiah 1 – 39*, Louisville: Westminster/John Knox Press, 1998

Brueggemann, Walter, *Isaiah 40 – 66*, Louisville: Westminster/ John Knox Press, 1998

Brueggemann, Walter, *The Message of the Psalms: a Theological Commentary*, Minneapolis: Augsburg, 1984

Bryan, Cyril, P., *The Papyrus Ebers: translated from the Germon Version*, Appleton and Company: New York, 1931

Buck, Albert H., *The Growth of Medicine: from the Earliest Times to about 1800*, New Haven: Yale University Press, 1917

Bultema, Harry, *Commentary on Isaiah*, Grand Rapids, Michigan: Kregel Publications, 1981

Carley, Keith W., *The Book of the Prophet Ezekiel*, Cambridge, England: Cambridge University Press, 1974

Carroll, Robert P., *Jeremiah: a Commentary*, Philadelphia: The Westminster Press, 1986

Childs, Brevard S., *The Book of Exodus, a Critical and Theological Commentary*, Louisville: the Westminster Press, 1974

Clifford, Richard J., *Proverbs: a Commentary*, Louisville: Westminster/John Knox Press, 1999

Coggins, R.J., *The Books of Ezra and Nehemiah*, New York:

Cambridge University Press, 1976

Cole, the Rev. Canon R.A., *The Gospel According to Mark: an Introduction and Commentary*, Grand Rapids, Michigan: William B. Eerdmans Publishing Company, 1989

Cooley's Cyclopedia of Practical Receipts and Collateral Information in the Arts, Manufactures, Professions, and Trades including Medicine, Pharmacy, Hygiene, and Domestic Economy designed as a Comprehensive Supplement to the Pharmacopoeia and General Book of Reference for the Manufacturer, Tradesman, Amateur and Heads of Families, volumes 1 and 2, Seventh edition, W. North, ed., London: J and A Churchill, 1892

Crenshaw, James L., *Ecclesiastes: a Commentary*, Philadelphia: Westminster Press, 1987

Culpepper, Nicholas, *The English Physician, enlarged, with Three Hundred and Sixty-nine medicines, made of English Herbs, that were not in any impression until this*, Gainsborough: printed by and for Henry Mozley, 1813

Dawson, Warren R., *Clio Medica – a Series of Primers on the History of Medicine*, E.B. Krumbhaar, ed., *the Beginnings – Egypt and Assyria*, New York: Paul B. Hoeber, Inc., 1930

Dawson, Warren R., *Magician and Leech: a Study in the Beginnings of Medicine with Special Reference to Ancient Egypt*, London: Methuen and Company, Ltd., 1919

Dibelius, Martin, *A Commentary on the Epistle of James*, Philadelphia: Fortress Press, 1976

Duke, James A., *Herbs of the Bible - 2000 Years of Plant Medi-*

cine, Loveland, Colorado: Interweave Press, 1999

Dunglison, Richard J., *History of Medicine from the Earliest Ages to the Commencement of the Nineteenth Century*, Philadelphia: Lindsay and Blakeston, 1872

Dunn, James D.G., *The Acts of the Apostles*, Valley Forge, Pennsylvania: Trinity Press International, 1996

Eichrodt, Walter, *Ezekiel: a Commentary*, London: SCM Ltd., 1970

Fee, Gordon D., *Paul's Letter to the Philippians*, Grand Rapids, Michigan: William B. Eerdmans Publishing Company, 1995

Fischer-Rizzi, Susanne, *The Complete Incense Book*, New York: Sterling Publishing Company, Incorporated, 1996

Ford, J. Massyngberde, *The Anchor Bible: Revelation*, Garden City, New York: Doubleday & Company, Incorporated, 1975

Fox, Michael V., *Character and Ideology in the Book of Esther*, Columbia, South Carolina: University of South Carolina Press, 1991

Garrison, Fielding H., *An Introduction to the History of Medicine with Medical Chronology, Suggestions for Study and Bibliographic Data*, Philadelphia: W.B. Saunders, Company, 1929

Geldenhuys, Norval, *Commentary on the Gospel of Luke: the English Text with Introduction, Exposition and Notes*, Grand Rapids, Michigan: William B. Eerdmans Publishing Company, 1977

Gerstenberger, Erhard S., *Leviticus: a Commentary*, Louisville:

Westminster/John Knox Press, 1993

Grieve, M., *A Modern Herbal: the Medicinal, Culinary, Cosmetic and Economic Properties, Cultivation and Folk-lore of Herbs, Grasses, Fungi, Shrubs & Trees with All Their Modern Scientific Uses, Volumes 1 and 2*, New York: Dover Publications, Incorporated, 1971

Gunther, Robert T., *The Greek Herbal of Dioscorides: Illustrated by a Byzantine AD 512, Englished by John Goodyear, AD 1655, edited and first printed AD 1933*, Oxford: Oxford University Press, 1934

Habel, Norman C., *The Book of Job: a Commentary*, Philadelphia: The Westminster Press, 1985

Harpur, Tom, *The Uncommon Touch: an Investigation of Spiritual Healing*, Toronto, Ontario: McClelland and Stewart Incorporated, 1994

Harvey, Van A., *A Handbook of Theological Terms*, New York: The Macmillan Company, 1964

Hepper, F. Nigel, *Baker Encyclopedia of Bible Plants: Flowers and Trees, Fruits and Vegetables Ecology*, Grand Rapids, Michigan: Baker Book House, 1992

Hertzberg, Hans Wilhelm, *I and II Samuel: A Commentary*, Philadelphia: The Westminster Press, 1964

Hillers, Dilbert R., *Micah: a Commentary on the Book of the Prophet Micah*, Philadelphia: Fortress Press, 1984

Holy Bible, The, Containing the Old and New Testaments, King James Version, Nashville: Thomas Nelson Publishers, 1989

Hooker, Morna , *The Gospel According to Saint Mark*, London: Hendrickson Publishing Incorporated, 1991

Huson, Paul, *Mastering Herbalism: a Practical Guide*, New York: Stein and Day Publishers, 1974

Interpreter's Bible, The: The Holy Scriptures in the King James and Revised Standard Versions with General Articles and Introduction, Exegesis, Exposition for Each Book of the Bible, Volumes 1,2,3,4,5,6,7,8,9,10,11,12, Nashville: Abingdon Press, 1952

Interpreter's Dictionary of the Bible, The: An Illustrated Encyclopedia Identifying and Explaining All Proper Names and Significant Terms and Subjects in the Holy Scriptures, Including the Apocrypha, with Attention to Archaeological Discoveries and Researches into the Life and Faith of Ancient Times, Volumes 1,2,3,4, Nashville: Abingdon Press, 1962

Janzen, J. Gerald, *Exodus*, Louisville: Westminster/John Knox Press, 1997

Jeremias, Jorg, *The Book of Amos: a Commentary*, Louisville: Westminster/John Knox Press, 1995

Keel, Othmar, *The Song of Songs: a Continental Commentary*, Minneapolis: Fortress Press, 1994

Kelsey, Morton, *Healing and Christianity: a Classic Study*, Minneapolis: Augsburg, 1995

Kestemaker, Simon J., *Exposition of the Second Epistle to the Corinthians*, Grand Rapids, Michigan: William B. Eerdmans Publishing Company, 1997

Knight, George A.F., *Hosea*, London: SCM Press, 1960

Knight, George A.F., *Psalms – the Daily Study Bible, volumes 1 and 2*, Philadelphia: Westminster Press, 1981 (volume 1), 1982 (volume 2)

Ladd, George Eldon, *A Commentary on the Revelation of John*, Grand Rapids, Michigan: William B. Eerdmans Publishing Company, 1972

Leyel, Mrs. C.F., *The Magic of Herbs: a Modern Book of Secrets*, New York: Harcourt, Brace and Company, 1926

Ligeros, Kleanthes A., *How Ancient Healing Governs Modern Medicine: the Contribution of Hellenic Science to Modern Medicine and Scientific Progress*, New York: G.P. Putnam's Son, 1937

Lindars, Barnabas, editor, *The Gospel of John*, London: Oliphants, 1972

Lloyd, John Ur, *Origin and History of all the Pharmacopeial Vegetable Drugs with Bibliography*, Cincinnati: The Caxton Press, 1929

Longman III, Tremper, *The Book of Ecclesiastes*, Grand Rapids, Michigan: William B. Eerdmans Publishing Company, 1998

Maier, Walter A., *The Book of Nahum: a Commentary*, St. Louis: Concordia Publishing House, 1959

Marshall, I. Howard, *The Acts of the Apostles: an Introduction and Commentary*, Grand Rapids, Michigan: William B. Eerdmans Publishing Company, 1980

Martin, Ralph P., *The Epistle of Paul to the Philippians*, Grand Rapids, Michigan: William B. Eerdmans Publishing Company, 1959

Maxwell, Marcus, *Revelation*, New York: Doubleday, 1998

Mayes. A.D.H., *Deuteronomy- New Century Bible Commentary*, Grand Rapids, Michigan: William b. Eerdmans Publishing Company, 1979

Mays, James Luther, *Amos: a Commentary*, London: SCM Press, 1969

Mays, James Luther, *Hosea: a Commentary*, London: SCM Press, 1969

Mays, James Luther, *Micah: a Commentary*, Philadelphia: The Westminster Press, 1976

Meyer, Joseph E., *The Herbalist*, Hammond, Indiana: Indiana Botanic Gardens, 1934

Mitton, C. Leslie, *Ephesians*, London: Oliphants, 1976

Mitton, C. Leslie, *Epistle of James, The*, Grand Rapids, Michigan: William B. Eerdmans Publishing Company, 1966

Morris, Leon, *The Gospel According to John: the English Text with Introduction, Exposition and Notes*, Grand Rapids, Michigan: William B. Eerdmans Publishing Company, 1971

Murphy, Roland E., *The Song of Songs: a Commentary on the Book of Canticles or the Song of Songs*, Minneapolis: Fortress Press, 1990

Nelson's Complete Concordance of the RSV Bible, New York: Thomas Nelson and Sons, 1957

Noordtzij, A., *Numbers*, Grand Rapids, Michigan: Zondervan Publishing House, 1983

Oxford Annotated Bible with the Apocrypha, The, Revised Standard Version, Herbert G. May and Bruce M. Metzger, editors, New York: Oxford University Press, 1965

Omanson, Roger L., and John Ellengton, *Paul's Second Letter to the Corinthians*, New York: United Bible Society Handbook Series, 1993

Panos, Maesimund B., M.D., and Jane Heimlich, *Homeopathic Medicine at Home: Natural Remedies for Everyday Ailments and Minor Injuries*, New York: Penguin Putnam, Inc., 1980

Paterson, Wilma, *A Fountain of Gardens: Plants and Herbs of the Bible*, Edinburgh, Scotland; Mainstream Publishing Company, Ltd., 1990

Patte, Daniel, *The Gospel According to Matthew: a Structural Commentary on Matthew's Gospel*, Valley Forge, Pennsylvania: Trinity Press International, 1987

Pfitzner, Victor C., *Hebrews*, Nashville: Abingdon Press, 1997

Pope, Marvin H., *The Anchor Bible: Song of Songs - a New Translation with Introduction and Commentary*, Garden City, New York: Doubleday & Company, Incorporated, 1977

Porteous, Norman W., *Daniel*, London: SCM Press Ltd., 1965

Price, Shirley, *Aromatherapy Workbook: Understanding Essential*

Oils from Plant to Bottle, Wellingborough, England: Thorsons, 1993

Price, Shirley and Len Price, *Aromatherapy for Health Professionals*, Philadelphia: Churchill Livingstone, 1999

Reyburn, William D., *A Handbook on Lamentations*, New York: United Bible Society, 1992

Riggans, Walter, *Numbers – the Daily Study Bible, Old Testament*, Philadelphia: Westminster Press, 1983

Roberts, J.J.M., *Nahum, Habakkuk, and Zephaniah: a Commentary*, Louisville: Westminster/John Knox Press, 1991

Rose, Jeanne, *Aromatherapy Studies Course by Correspondence*, San Francisco: Jeanne Rose Aromatherapy, 2001

Rose, Jeanne, *The Aromatherapy Book: Applications & Inhalations*, Berkeley: North Atlantic Books, 1992

Rose, Jeanne, *Herbal Body Book: the Herbal Way to Natural Beauty & Health for Men & Women*, Berkeley: Frog, Limited, 2000

Rose, Jeanne, *375 Essential Oils and Hydrosols*, Berkeley: Frog, Limited, 1999

Samuel; Introduction, Revised Version with Notes, Index and Maps, Rev. A.R.S. Kennedy, editor, New York: Henry Frowche, 1905

Schnaubelt, Kurt, *Advanced Aromatherapy: the Science of Essential Oil Therapy*, Rochester, Vermont: Healing Arts Press, 1998

Schweizer, Eduard, *The Good News According to Luke*, Atlanta: John Knox Press, 1984

Schweizer, Eduard, *The Good News According to Matthew*, Atlanta: John Knox Press, 1975

Scott, R.B.Y., *The Anchor Bible: Proverbs - Ecclesiastes*, Garden City, New York: Doubleday & Company, Incorporated, 1965

Seelig, Major G., *Medicine: an Historical Outline*, Baltimore: Williams and Wilkins Company, 1925

Shewell-Cooper, W.E., *Plants, Flowers and Herbs of the Bible: the Living Legacy of the Third Day of Creation*, New Canaan, Connecticut: Keats Publishing, Inc., 1977

Singer, Charles, *A Short History of Medicine: Introducing Medical Principles to Students and Non-medical Readers*, New York: Oxford University Press (American branch), 1928

Sloyan, Gerard, *Interpretation: a Bible Commentary for Teaching and Preaching - John*, Atlanta: John Knox Press, 1988

Thomson, William A.R., editor, *Medicines from the Earth: a Guide to Healing Plants*, Maidenhead, England: McGraw-Hill Book Company (UK) Limited, 1978

Throckmorton, Jr., Burton H., *Gospel Parallels: a Synopsis of the First Three Gospels with Alternative Readings from the Manuscripts and Noncanonical Parallels*, Nashville: Thomas Nelson Publishers, 1979

Tissarand, Robert and Tony Balacs, *Essential Oil Safety: a Guide for Health Care Professionals*, Philadelphia: Churchill Livingstone, 1995

Turner, Laurence A., *Genesis*, Sheffield, England: Sheffield Academic Press, 2000

Von Rad, Gerhard, *Genesis: a Commentary*, Philadelphia: Westminster Press, 1972

Walker, Winifred, *All the Plants of the Bible*, New York: Harper and Brothers Publishers, 1957

Waserman, Manfred and Samuel S. Kolteck, eds., *Health and Disease in the Holy Land: Studies in the History and Sociology of Medicine from Ancient Times to the Present*, Lewiston, New York: The Edwin Millen Press, 1996

Weiser, Artur, *The Psalms - a Commentary*, Philadelphia: The Westminster Press, 1962

Wilder, Alexander, *History of Medicine: a Brief Outline of Medical History and Sects of Physicians, from the Earliest Historic Period; with an Extended Account of the New Schools of the Healing Art in the Nineteenth Century*, New Sharon, Maine: New England Eclectic Publishing Company, 1901

Williamson, Jr., Lamar, *Interpretation: a Bible Commentary for Teaching and Preaching - Mark*, Louisville: John Knox Press, 1983

Wiseman, Donald J., *1 and 2 Kings: an Introduction and Commentary*, Downers Grove, Illinois: Inter Varsity Press, 1993

Wolff, Hans Walter, *Joel and Amos: a Commentary on the Books of the Prophets Joel and Amos*, Philadelphia: Fortress Press, 1977

World Book Encyclopedia, volumes 3,8,9,13, Chicago: World

Book Incorporated, 1994

Worwood, Valerie Ann, *The Complete Book of Essential Oils & Aromatherapy*, San Rafael, California: New World Library, 1991

Worwood, Valerie Ann, *The Fragrant Mind: Aromatherapy for Personality, Mind, Mood, and Emotion*, Novato, California: New World Library, 1996

Worwood, Valerie Ann, *The Fragrant Heavens: the Spiritual Dimension of Fragrance and Aromatherapy*, Novato, California: New World Library, 1999

Worwood, Valerie Ann, *The Fragrant Pharmacy: a Complete Guide to Aromatherapy & Essential Oils*, New York: Bantam Books, 1990

Worwood, Valerie Ann, *Scents & Scentuality: Aromatherapy & Essential Oils for Romance, Love, and Sex*, Novato, California: New World Library, 1999

Young, Edward J., *A Commentary on Daniel*, London: the Banner of Truth Trust, 1949

Internet-Website Sources

Aromatherapy - A Brief History
www.cris.com/~bluerose/aic/history.htm
copyright@1996
by Blue Corp Industries Incorporated

AromaWeb™, www.aromaweb.com the following articles/
information:
Hazardous Essential Oils
Cinnamon
History of Aromatherapy
Oil Profiles
Spikenard
What are Essential Oils?

Doctrine of Signatures
Eds.mounet.com/~jdye/doctrine.html
Egypt, History of – Dynasties
Home.rmi.net/~grymntl/bos/herb/doctsig.html
www.touregypt.net/ehistory.html

Galen
www.med.virginia.edu/hs-library

Hammurabi, the Code of
www.campus.northpark.edu/history/WebChron/MiddleEast/
HammurabiCode.html

Health World Online, www.healthy.net
"A History of Fragrance" which was excerpted from:
Keville, Kathi and Mindy Green, *Aromatherapy: A Complete Guide to the Healing Art*, Freedom, California: Crossing Press, 1995

Herbalism, Western
Gale Encyclopedia of Alternative Health Medicine
www.findarticles.com/cf-o/g2603/00 . . .

Hippocrates
www.allsands.com/Science/hippocratesbiog_rtb_gn.html

Imhotep
Interoz.com/egypt/who/imhotep.html

Kyphi
Kyphi Essentials
www.kyphi.com.au/pages/about.html

Vanhove, Michael, Aromatherapy
www.nature-helps.com/infopage/engels/intro.htm
Introduction
Essential oil components
History of aromatherapy

Printed in the United States
890100002B